COOK YOUR
Marriage
HAPPY

COOK YOUR
Marriage
HAPPY

Debra Borden, LCSW

The Sous Therapist

CYH PRESS

FIRST EDITION

ISBN: 978-0-9998718-0-5

Dedication

Nothing I do in life means more to me than the health
and happiness of my children. I truly believe that "I cook them happy."
At least they seem to keep coming back for more! I'm so grateful for that.
Erika, David and Jamie: this book is for you.

This book could not have been created without the love, affection,
and support of one person: Dr. Nyman, Sir. (Enjoy that, David,
it's a one-time thing—with a very short shelf-life.) Thank you.
With love and gratitude. For everything.

Acknowledgements

This book would not have been possible without the talent and genius of Steve Bennett and the entire AuthorBytes team.

To Jackie Mitchard: I'm inspired by your writing, humbled by your knowledge, and working with you was both a lesson and a gift. In short, you've edited me happy.

To the communities of therapists and writers: generosity of spirit is our strength. I cherish your brilliance and perspective and I thank you for allowing me to believe I'm a part of both.

To Mitch Margo, fellow author and friend, you helped me to reclaim my voice.

As always, a special shout out to Jayne and Robin, my reality checks, who talk me happy.

To all my extended family and the limbs of Feldmans, Bordens, Petaks, Pearsons, Buraks, and Nymans. As I always say, branches only bloom when the trunk of the tree is strong. Thanks to you, I bow but don't break.

To new friends and old; these days each year seems to bring the gift of new people and bonds with longtime friends that grow stronger. You sustain me.

To my colleagues in Addiction Treatment who know that when we help others we help ourselves even more: your dedication reminds me to strive to be my biggest self.

To the communities of readers and foodies, what a fabulous and fun group we are, finding adventure and excitement in our own kitchens and backyards. We are so lucky. I am so grateful to be in the group.

Author's Note

A great team of professionals helped me to construct and refine the manuscript and recipes for this book. You will note that almost every time I mention a recipe there is a way to find it in one of the appendices. Recipes that we do 'in session' are also in their own appendix as well as in the body of the text.

As a home cook I'd like to apologize in advance for any missteps in either ingredients or (gasp!) shameful shortcuts that might cause highly trained chefs, who have my complete adoration, to roll their eyes. Forgive me!

—DB, *The Sous Therapist*

Table of Contents

How to Use This Book

Please note that *Cook Your Marriage Happy* is divided into specific therapy sessions, each with their own three recipes. These are *SESSION RECIPES* and can be found both in the session and in alphabetical order in Appendix A, Session Recipes, at the back of the book.

Additionally, for your convenience, every recipe mentioned, even if not used in session, is called an *EXTRA RECIPE*, and can be found, in alphabetical order, in Appendix B, Extra Recipes. When you become adept at Cooking Therapy you can try any of these recipes as your own session.

I hope you will!

Amuse-Bouche
(Or How I Became a Sous Therapist)

A few years ago, I was in my friend Jenna's kitchen as she prepared lunch for her four-year-old, Kyle, a child who used to average about eighty-two questions every ten minutes, and that day, Kyle was on a high-speed riff.

"You always loved me, right Mommy?"

"Yes, Kyle. Absolutely."

"You loved me even before I was born?"

Jenna and I chuckled, before she answered, "Even before you were born."

"Even when I was in your tummy?"

"Yes Kyle, I loved you even when you were in my tummy."

"And you loved me before that, when I was still food?"

At that, Jenna and I stared at her little boy, both of us speechless.

What?

Of course, Kyle assumed that in order for him to have ended up in his mom's tummy, she had to have *eaten* him! Now that was amusing. But I never forgot the story.

Years later I find myself remembering it and wondering if this precocious little kid wasn't on to something after all – several things, in fact. In addition to wondering about babies, Kyle, in anticipation of his delectable grilled cheese sandwich, must have made an association between love and food, as well as hunger and desire. All of us can relate to that. Everyone has a memory of a perfect meal that somehow has never been duplicated, even with the same ingredients or a visit to the same restaurant. Upon further exploration, you often learn that while it may have been delicious Rigatoni Bolognese or Duck à l'Orange, more than likely the company was special and the emotion, anything from camaraderie to peace to lust, contributed to the perfectly cooked pasta or "best sauce ever." In fact, I know one couple who reminisce about a late-night snack as they describe the date where they knew their relationship was getting serious. They both tell the same story.

"The eggs at that diner were better than any we'd ever had. We both wondered if they might be raising organic chickens!"

In downtown Passaic, New Jersey? Not likely. But the feeling of the moment made the meal special. And the couple moved in together just a month after that meal.

Even the smell of food brings back memories of love. For me, parsley means that if I peek into the kitchen my grandmother will be making soup. No matter that she's been gone for thirty years! And cumin became my BFF at a vulnerable time. The smell will always remind me of an actual chunk of time in my life when I felt challenged and ultimately supported.

When I think about Cooking Therapy I know it's a perfect fit as one piece of our universal search for sense of self. These days, we are all more focused on uncovering the essence of who we are, through mediums like meditation or travel or analysis. Often the journey to understanding involves our senses – what we see, touch, and even taste.

As for me, I might ask myself, who was I before I was me? Before I was a writer and a therapist and a wife and mother? Before I was a lover of Broadway musicals and cheesy biographies and even cheesier Danish pastries? Before I learned that I'm resilient and courageous but also imperfect and flawed and have (almost) learned to live with that!

Unlike Kyle, I never thought that I started out as a grilled cheese sandwich. But if I had to guess what I was "even before," as he put it, I have no doubt that I was one of those jolly, plump, English cooks bringing trays of scones and tea to her lady mistress and shouting orders to the scullery maids like, "Madam is feeling a bit out of temper. Do bring me the plums for pudding!" (Full Disclosure: I do not know exactly what a scullery maid is, but I'm sure I would have employed at least two.)

For years, I paid no attention to the fact that I'd been using cooking as a way to organize, manage, and either emotionally excavate or soothe my experiences. When I really took time to consider it, I recalled that, even as a young girl, I concocted snacks intended to assuage my moods. My favorite was a triple-decker cream cheese and jelly sandwich that I rarely finished. (I mean, who could finish a triple-decker cream cheese and jelly sandwich, no matter *how* distraught not to be in the popular crowd?) Still, it was never about the eating but instead the process – the assembling. Somehow, all the angst of a school day could be spread, then stacked and finally, sliced and savored away.

When my first child went off to college, I instinctively began to ship him baked banana breads and chocolate cheesecake muffins.

I did this even though he was attending school in Madison, Wisconsin, the cheese and pastry capitol of the world! Of course, the point wasn't really sending him snacks: I was trying to work out my own longing for him through the process of cookery. Those delectable treats were intended more to comfort me than him, as the name of the recipe implies: Miss You Mucho Mini Muffins.

If you'd like to try making Miss You Mucho Mini Muffins at any time, you won't be disappointed. An old family recipe that freezes well, the muffins are mini but the result is always a gigantic hit. See Extra Recipes, Appendix B.

From that moment on I also began to name my recipes purposefully because language is so powerful. There's even a science called Neuro-Linguistic Programming that studies the effects that words have on our mood and mindset. In simple terms, think of the person who says, "I can't" and replace that statement with "Usually I don't." One is finite, the other has possibility.

Now I realize that whenever I'm sad I need to bake. Sometimes, I bake for days.

If the sadness is due to a real or perceived failure, the recipes I choose are often complicated or new. "Complicated" provides a sense of purpose and mastery. A version of Dulce de Leche Cake does the trick. I've customized the recipe so I can literally go from boiling to freezing in the same recipe; what a tangible metaphor! Dulce de leche literally means boiling down milk and sugar to create something else, so I call my recipe From Boiling to Bliss Cake. *Feel up to a challenge? (You will after our sessions together). Then dig in to this modified version of dulce de leche from Bon Appetit. See Extra Recipes, Appendix B.*

If the sadness is more free-floating, or due to boredom, a few simple steps might be enough to provide distraction. A No-Bake Icebox Cake using Nabisco chocolate cookies is not only easy but looks impressive.

We will actually use this next recipe in session later on. I call it Chill on it Icebox Cake and also You Are Not an Icebox Cake, depending on the issue we address. But the recipe is the same.

Chill on it Icebox Cake (aka You Are Not an Icebox Cake) is an easy-peasy no-bake way to brighten any day. Chill out with the recipe in Extra Recipes, Appendix B.

Even a chocolate pudding pie with ladyfingers and whipped cream can be enough to change my mood. I've always thought of whipped cream as a happy food. Call me crazy, but there's something about those frothy peaks that lifts your spirit! On a side note, this recipe was taught to me by my mother-in-law Helen Borden, may she rest in peace. It's not lost on me that a happy dessert should come from a mother-in-law, a group that often gets a bad rap. This is a group I'm especially sensitive to, because I've recently become a part of it! Yay moms-in-law!

Don't worry about making Don't Worry Be Happy Pie – this old family recipe takes minimal effort but satisfies to the max! De-stress with the recipe in Extra Recipes, Appendix B.

Conversely, after I was published for the first time, feeling confident and validated, I began to attack recipes from the cover of *Gourmet Magazine* or tackle California Rolls from scratch.

You'll be rolling in self-pride and applause when you roll out Just Roll with it Dude California Rolls. See Extra Recipes, Appendix B.

Every mood seems to dictate a particular type of cuisine. Frustrated? Bring on the chopped salad. Lazy? It's soups and stews. And when I feel sexy I go for sauces, especially cream sauces.

No, I don't know what that means. Well, not completely.

Here is a simple one for Besame (Kiss Me!) Bechamel. They'll all want to kiss the cook after tasting your Besame (Kiss Me) Béchamel. See Extra Recipes, Appendix B.

Eventually I realized that cooking might have a place in my clinical practice, especially with clients who might have a hard time in the one-on-one, direct dyad. For all therapeutic breakthroughs, even mini ones, clarifying the root of an emotion can be a first step. For me, clarifying that cooking was an actual therapy was just that; the first step to helping others do the same.

I now realize that this was a skill I learned as a young child although I do *not* come from a long line of great cooks. In fact, it's probably fair to say I've exceeded the mostly maternal cooking talents of my family. *But*, the moods my family teachers could change, create, and inspire were top notch. Nanny standing at the stove, frying potato pancakes or bacon, letting them drain on paper towels knowing full well that grandchildren (even adult ones) would be "stealing" them before they cooled? This was great fun made more delicious as she pretended to swipe our hands away, somehow just missing us every time. And my mom, lifting first me, and years later, my young children, onto the kitchen counter to help make a simple fruit salad. We couldn't use a knife but we could sure plop in the berries and grapes and "paint" the counter with raspberry juice.

So, it occurred to me that the feelings of safety and solace I'd learned for myself and my family could be transferred to some of my more reticent clients, especially adolescents. These me-focused beings often resented being "sent" to therapy at all, and certainly had no stake in utilizing the "me time" that was costing their parents money and costing them precious computer or phone time. Engaging them was a challenge. I often played games, or took walks, or created other activities that would engage their interest and foster expression, while at the same time promoting an atmosphere of safety. Couple that with the memories of warmth I had around being in the kitchen and preparing food, and I knew that it would help immeasurably with developing rapport, so important in the therapeutic relationship.

And so, in the same vein of art or music therapy, another legitimate modality emerged: Cooking Therapy.

It was so successful it was scary.

The families I visited as a therapist ran the gamut from extremely economically challenged to extremely financially advantaged. In both situations, as a therapist, I was always meticulously conscious of making sure that I didn't present myself as some sort of hero due to the tangible "gift" of food. Although I always brought the ingredients, and in homes where resources were limited brought my own cookware, I always took half the "bounty" home with me so that my clients felt there was an equality between us. I never wanted either client to feel as if they were "poor" in any way and in need of charity.

Here is an example of a day that describes the almost schizophrenic experience of working with clients at both ends of the economic spectrum.

In the morning, I visit a basement apartment in a subsidized housing complex to work through feelings of distress with an eleven-year old girl (let's call her Rayna) who is in trouble for leaving cookie crumbs on the floor and "so the rats came again." As Rayna put it, her mom "went ballistic" and now she was punished; no TV for two days.

That afternoon I arrive at the palatial home of a very wealthy family and spend a good deal of the session helping seventeen-year old twin boys (Justin and Jordan) process their feelings about learning that when they pass their driver's tests, instead of each getting their own Range Rover, they will have to share just one. And boy are they pissed.

As you can see, the mandate for a therapist to "leave your own biases at the door," is a constant challenge. In both cases, despite the great disparity of situation, Cooking Therapy helped diffuse negative emotions and made it easier to discuss issues like fairness, perspective, responsibility, and gratitude. In this case, it was less about the recipe and more about engaging in an activity that didn't require eye contact. So often, clients who feel "wrong" feel shame and become defensive if confronted, even gently, face to face. With these clients, diffusing the discussion with an activity promoted more self-examination, and eventually got Rayna to understand her piece in the problem and the boys to at least explore the idea of entitlement. By the way, in both cases we made cupcakes. Cupcakes offer an awful lot of choice (flavor, fillings, and toppings) for the client/cook. While these two homes may have seemed worlds apart, feelings of being out of control were actually common to both. We made Your Cup of Tea Cupcakes and you can too.

Go wild or mild with your choice of toppings for Your Cup of Tea Cupcakes. See Extra Recipes, Appendix B. This is a basic cupcake recipe from Real Simple. You get to customize the additions and toppings.

Here are other examples:

Sixteen-year-old Anna plunged her hands into chopped meat as if to mash away the resentment of her mother's long hours and her father's absence. By the time we had meatballs (sweet n' sour, of course, you have to mine the metaphors whenever possible) she'd said more than in three other sessions combined.

Nothing mirrors life more than these Life is Sweet and Sour Meatballs. Remind yourself by making them. See Extra Recipes, Appendix B.

Twelve-year-old Gabe, the youngest member of a newly blended family, would watch his new step-siblings get picked up by their dad, then wait for his biological mother to come for him, which almost never happened. As I watched him use the hand mixer to beat eggs I had the sense that along with the batter, a good chunk of his frustration was also turning from liquid to froth; he simply became lighter.

This is not to say that there haven't been mishaps. There have, of course. I remember the time I brought shrimp to a client who kept Kosher (the cleaning and shelling was to mirror moving on – and so it did with me, right out of the house) or the Chocolate Pudding planned to model patience for a young client with ADHD (the thickening took so long he left me in the kitchen and went to play Xbox).

Still, the successes have outnumbered the failures. And in both fiascos, I did manage to reframe "disaster" as an opportunity to discuss embarrassment, mistakes (grownups and even therapists do make them – surprise!), and perspective. I'm told the Chinese sign for crisis is made up of two smaller signs: one for danger and one for opportunity. I like that. And while some say that this description of Chinese characters is a myth, I like it anyway!

Building on my work with teens, I then incorporated the same principles into my work with all ages, genders, and a variety of issues. I've always gravitated toward "brief" or "solution-focused" therapy, which gives great hope to a client. Contracting for attainable goals (just like attempting a recipe!) suits my personal style which has always been more guide than director, more Sherpa than surgeon. *Together,* we embark on a clear, step-by-step journey of insight and thoughtfulness.

Preparing a dish is the simplest, most pared-down example of this.

Sift flour. Add water. Stir together. Bake.

Who knows? We might end up with bread. Or a sense of ourselves. Maybe both.

To my satisfaction, since I've touted Cooking Therapy for years, it's gratifying to see the medical research beginning to catch up. In December 2014, the *Wall Street Journal* featured an article by Jeannie Whalen about the benefits of cooking as therapy.

"Experts are increasingly turning to Cooking Therapy for patients in need," Whalen reports, "Cooking Therapy is being used to treat Substance Abuse, Depression, and Schizophrenia."

So too, many schools, behavioral institutions, and senior centers are incorporating cooking into their programs. A recent clinical study published by UNCG for the *Journal of Recreational Therapy* regarding the benefits of cooking for the elderly reported the following:

"Food and the act of cooking — have powerful meaning to older adults. Food defines culture, family history, and traditions. For many, cooking signifies basic worth, self-image, and role identity. Food is also connected with feelings of love, pleasure and enjoyment, holidays, celebrations, family, and spirituality. The product of cooking may be regarded as something to share, as family recipes often have a history attached to them. In traditional cultures, cooking, as a practical art, is passed down from mothers and grandmothers, to daughters and granddaughters with great pride. This ritual creates strong family relationship bonds." One facility where Cooking Therapy is incorporated into the programming is at the Atria Senior Living Centers.

Cooking Therapy can be utilized by all adults, regardless of age, and by adolescents too. CRC Health and Behavioral Health of the Palm Beaches are just two of the premier substance abuse and mental health facilities offering Culinary therapy to patients.

They attest: "For some, cooking is therapeutic. Culinary therapy encompasses cooking and cooking-related activities, such as cultivating a garden, planning and preparing meals, and educational grocery shopping and restaurant experiences. Under the supervision of a professional chef and/or therapist, patients learn about diet and nutrition and develop a healthy relationship with food."

And recently, *Psychology Today* recognized that "Kitchen Therapy" may be "Cooking Up Mental Well Being." Linda Wasmer Andrews writes:

"Now culinary therapy is the treatment du jour at a growing number of mental health clinics and therapists' offices. It's being used as part of the treatment for a wide range of mental and behavioral health conditions, including depression, anxiety, eating disorders, ADHD and addiction."

In the therapeutic community, it's common knowledge that hands-on, tangible acts are often highly effective treatment components for many kinds of emotional issues. While all sorts of these creative therapies are effective, they are not always readily available. For example, Equine Therapy is a highly emotional, mostly non-verbal therapeutic modality. In recent years, its popularity has soared. While once a boutique or "extra" service, dozens of facilities and treatment programs now offer Equine Therapy as part of their regular programming. You don't have to be in an inpatient program to take advantage of Equine Therapy, but you do need to be within striking distance of a satellite location, and by definition this is usually in a rural setting or at least one where horses can thrive. As you can imagine, the cost can be considerable too. One thing we do know is that utilization of treatment rises with ease of accessibility, and vice versa, making Equine Therapy, though powerful, often difficult to obtain.

While the two are quite different, many of the same emotions can be conjured up in both Cooking Therapy and Equine Therapy; surrender, nurture, calm, clarity, and focus. Cooking Therapy can serve as a tool to examine your behaviors and bring them into consciousness. Things you do in the kitchen or with a recipe are often remarkably telling about how you address the relationships and challenges or obstacles in your life. In Equine Therapy, similar patterns are explored. And that's the beauty of a concrete therapy. With guided prompts and process, you can uncover your strengths and barriers in a strong, tangible way, something that may take longer in a traditional talk therapy session.

To further illustrate, think of it this way: you go to England and you know that you need to drive on the other side of the street. You may even think about it in your head and remind yourself that you need to look right-left-right instead of the opposite way you've learned and driven for years. When you make a turn, you again tell yourself that you'll have to turn into the left lane and not the right. You go over it with your friends. You've got this, right? But nothing can prepare you for when you're actually in the car, at the wheel. And the first time you do it incorrectly and the horns are blaring and other drivers are cursing and you almost have a head-on collision? Very, very different from the story you told yourself in your head.

By the way, the first time I did Equine Therapy I cried in front of colleagues, so trust me about the power of a tangible experience.

As I mentioned, there is a proven correlation between difficulty of access and non-access. As one increases, so does the other. In other words, if it's too far or too expensive a client is not likely to go or keep going. Food is utilitarian; readily available and generally affordable and, at the end of a session, you not only get the beginnings of emotional health, but the beginnings of dinner! This may sound funny but there is truth in the humor. If you can mine an activity to do double duty, wouldn't you? Just as your long drive gives you the chance to catch up on an audio book, why not attempt to get a bit of emotional fiber out of those sesame noodles?

Here is a long-time go-to recipe for me, Sesame Noodles from *The Silver Palate Cookbook*, that I've renamed, Sesame NEWdles. Like this recipe, we evolve. That's a good thing. ***Prepare these NEWdles, to simulate that change is okay and for a lighter, healthier, you. See Extra Recipes, Appendix B.***

The spiritual benefits speak for themselves. Even Buddha said, "When you prepare your own food, you give to the food and the food gives back to you."

In the pages ahead I'll share with you the details, not only about how cooking has informed my practice, but, more importantly, how you might incorporate it into your own life, as a safe therapy that you can use on your own. *Yes, do try this at home!*

Throughout these pages you'll have me, The Sous Therapist as your guide.

Of course, while all cooking can be healing, nurturing, and empowering, Cooking Therapy is specific and purposeful. Though fun (and there's nothing wrong with that) and filled with stories, strategies and recipes, I employ Cooking Therapy as a legitimate therapeutic modality supported by a cognitive behavioral framework. In simple terms, this means we'll be looking at habits and behaviors that are either prompted or cemented by "self-talk;" the words in our head. We'll examine whether these words have helped or harmed us, and how they've been pivotal in shaping the way we behave.

So sit back, grab a spoon or a spatula, and learn how to cook pretty much any moment happy, whether it's coping with a new job or an old husband, an anxious child or obnoxious teen, an ailing dad or a nagging mother-in law! Together we'll craft a meal and a plan.

And by the end, you may realize, as I did, that it's entirely possible to cook yourself and your marriage happy.

Your session starts right now, with me, Debra Borden, LCSW, The Sous Therapist.

Note: As with other tangential therapies, Cooking Therapy is an adjunct to an overall therapeutic plan and should never replace traditional talk therapy, but rather, enhance and/or add to it. Although the author is a Licensed Clinical Social Worker and trained practitioner, this book is written in part with a light and entertaining style and sense of humor. You should always discuss any adjunct therapy with your personal psychotherapist.

COOK
YOURSELF
HAPPY®

Cook Your Marriage Happy!

Welcome to Cooking Therapy.

If you're wondering how Cooking Therapy can help improve your marriage, read on. (And don't worry, if you're a woman, the secret is not just making more morsels for your partner and it's *not* about putting all the pressure or responsibility for the *two* of you, on you!) Like Music, Art, or Equine therapies, Cooking Therapy is a tangible therapeutic modality that's now being used in a variety of clinical settings. Studies, including the one below from MIT, show that touch and sensory integration are recognized as important components of mental health. "Touch is fundamental to our emotional well-being. Medical science is starting to understand and develop touch-based therapies for autism spectrum, mood, anxiety, and borderline disorders."[1]

Additionally, tangible therapies can inspire breakthroughs or that "aha moment" you've heard of, in a way that traditional talk therapy may not – often in one session!

When I worked for a dual diagnosis treatment facility in Florida, the patients were able to participate in Surf Therapy. I know what you're thinking, because initially I was too; hokey, glitzy even, and more marketing than mental health. I couldn't have been more wrong. Done gender-specifically, with trained surfing staff and clinicians, patients spent a short amount of time in the shallow water near the beach learning to "surf." By surf, I don't mean to conjure up images of *Hawaii Five-0*. This was essentially managing to get on the board, possibly stand, and travel even a tiny bit...or not. Why was this a powerful and effective treatment? Some

1 Cati Vaucelle, Leonardo Bonanni, and Hiroshi Ishii. 2009. Design of haptic interfaces for therapy. In Proceedings of the 27th international conference on Human factors in computing systems (CHI '09). ACM, New York, NY, USA, 467-470.

of the participants came to the beach with intense anxiety (drowning), fears (sharks) and irrational beliefs (imminent tsunami). Many had simply never learned to swim or been in the ocean. And though frightening to some, we know that water can also be framed as nurturing and protective. It's womb-like, after all. Helping a patient to feel lighter and "buoyant" was often a bonus.

As you can also imagine, even a few steps into the water or a belly on the board was an accomplishment. Mastery is a feeling and result with legs; meaning, many of us give so much mental space to our failures but no equal time to our successes! Learning to let our accomplishments fill us with insight and pride promotes mental health. As with Cooking Therapy, the surfing was only part of the program, while the guided experience, the encouragement, the touch, reflection and process, rounded out the session.

Whether you've been married seven months or thirty-seven years, it's entirely normal to want to question, consider, and certainly improve your marriage.

In the next few pages we'll explore the four top marital complaints and cook our way through them. While no issue is completely resolved in one session, I promise you suggestions to "chew on" and strategies that will "take the bite out of" your concerns.

(For the sake of clarity, we will refer to *all* relationships between all types of couples as a kind of "marriage" from here on in.)

THE FOUR TOP MARITAL COMPLAINTS:

· The Sexually Out-of-Sync Marriage
· The Stale Marriage
· The Maybe-I-Made-a Mistake Marriage
· The Financially Frustrated Marriage

Chances are if you've read this far, your concerns fall into one or several of these categories. But I encourage you to read them all, as there is often an overlap between issues and strategies. Please know this one thing for sure: You are not alone in your concerns, and, just by starting to read, you've taken the most important step and often the hardest one. That step is simply showing up. As you've heard me say, ease of accessibility is the *single* biggest contributor to clients showing up, and showing up is the best way to begin the journey to a resolution.

One of the many benefits of Cooking Therapy is not only that it's easily accessible (your kitchen), but pocket-friendly (a meal often costing less than a single therapy session). It also does double duty because you get to eat your work! Another one of my sayings? Why not grab a side of self-esteem with that salmon?!

Toward that end, here is a recipe for crunchy wasabi salmon from Epicurious.com that I've renamed Salmon with a Side of Self Esteem. See Extra Recipes, Appendix B.

Before we go further, just a note about one prominent issue that shows up in couples counseling that I won't address here; adultery. While I believe that you can cook through many of the associated feelings of regret, anger, and resentment associated with cheating, this is deep couple's work that needs to be addressed with a highly-skilled professional. When trust is broken, and even if both members of the partnership are committed to moving forward, the intensity of the work is layered and complicated and requires a family and/or marital counselor.

Moving on to the four marital complaints! Let's assume that you also like to cook, or at least you're not totally turned off to it. But even if you are, don't worry, in every chapter, there is at least one recipe that has just a few easy steps. In fact, in each chapter you will have a choice of three recipes to make both with me and on your own.

There is a saying that therapy begins with the first phone call. That's because by reaching out you begin to acknowledge a problem, think about it, and bring it from a nagging, undecipherable worry to a manageable issue that can be tackled. Good for you! Because that's exactly what we're about to do. Roll up your sleeves, wash your hands, and let's begin!

Cook Your Sexually-Out-of-Sync Marriage Happy

So, what exactly *is* a sexually out-of-sync marriage? Well, first let's talk about what it *isn't* and what we won't address here:

We are not discussing hyper-sexuality, where one partner is clinically diagnosed with an elevated sex drive.

We are not discussing a sex addiction, which often focuses on stimuli other than the committed partnership.

We are not discussing fetishes or other seemingly unique sexual desires.

What we are focusing on is the most common scenario; a marriage where one partner consistently wants to have more sex than the other.

Years ago, I was asked to write an article for Dr. Oz's site, *realage.com*. The title of the article was "Frequency Discrepancy". One fact that should put you at ease is knowing that this website strives to hit a large demographic and thus, often focuses on problems that affect a large number of people. So, it's important to know that you are not alone and to toss out feelings of shame, guilt, or failure, just as you would that expired milk.

In other words, at one time or another and in most marriages, there is usually a discrepancy in how often each member of the couple wants to have sex, and there are a number of reasons, stages and events at the root, not all of them bad or wrong. But, when this discrepancy is consistent and long-lasting, and begins to cause stress for either or both of the individuals, it becomes an issue for the marriage.

This is a good time to remind my readers that Cooking Therapy can be a spark for clarity and/or self-evaluation. As with all tangible therapies, sometimes doing instead of talking can have different and powerful results. But a session of Cooking Therapy is not a cure-all. All marital issues will benefit from a trained facilitator of Couples Therapy, and issues related to sex respond especially well when addressed with a trained sex therapist. That said, I encourage you to read on and ultimately, cook on. You will be surprised at what you'll become aware of and learn.

First, some facts. Certified Sex Therapists report the following information:

Frequency discrepancy is the single biggest issue that brings couples to sex therapy!

What causes frequency discrepancy?

Disparity in sexual desire can be a sexual problem, a relationship problem, or both.

In terms of Cooking Therapy, the recipes and sessions that follow will address both.

It's not easy to talk about sexual dysfunction, but let's do just that. This kind of intimacy issue can take many shapes and should always be addressed first with a qualified physician. It may surprise you to know that 40% of women and 30% of men experience some type of sexual dysfunction that could be linked to a *physical cause*. Low libido, for example, may be due to chronic illness, medication, low testosterone level, or fatigue in both women and men.

And often, it can be corrected.

Let's start with the physical for now. Sometimes the female partner has never had an orgasm or can only have one by herself, which will of course eventually lead to frustration if not outright resentment and/or lack of interest on her part. Often this is simply due to poor or unimaginative foreplay.

Likewise, a man anxious about performance or maintaining an erection may try to avoid the act entirely. Many therapists work with couples to promote "goal-less" sex; going for pleasurable sensation rather than results to reduce pressure, increase connection, and ultimately, desire. Remember this when we get to our recipe and find pleasure in the process of cooking, even if the finished product never looks like the picture!

In Cooking Therapy, as in sex, we learn that the enjoyment of the act can be as satisfying as the end result! *No, really.*

One common physical issue that can quickly kill desire for a female partner is pain. To cope with that, vaginal moisturizers are available in stores, on the Internet and through your ob-gyn, and can be applied to both male and female genitals. How can Cooking Therapy possibly help with a problem like that?

Well, consider this story:

"I learned to bake from my mother, who used to send double and triple batches of chocolate brownies to my brother in the army. This was a long time ago before KitchenAids and Cuisinarts. I would help her cream the butter and sugar, always the first step. It was arduous enough if the butter was truly softened but sheer torture if it wasn't. We used the back of a wooden spoon, pressing the two ingredients together against the mixing bowl. For my mom, I think the elbow grease felt like love she was sending to her son. For me, it felt like annoying and painful servitude that my wrists, hands, and shoulders did not deserve. Let me add, once the brownies were done and had cooled, we then had to individually wrap each one in plastic wrap before placing them in aluminum foil and shoe boxes! Honestly, although the finished product was tasty, it never quite seemed worth it. Later in life, when I duplicated the recipe with electronic aid, somehow the brownies seemed more delicious! Perfectly dense and moist, a little crust on top, and no aching wrists!"

So, can you guess what's coming?

Yes, one of our sessions today will involve making brownies two ways; one with technology and one without. The end result will be a tangible lesson that there's no reason to get there painfully. Find the tools to make your "brownies" pleasurable and definitely pain-free. And remember, that pleasure might be just as surprising to you as it was for my brother, who I'm sure brightened considerably as he opened up those boxes of love in a faraway place. He was feeling lonely and disconnected – you know, kind of like you or your partner might feel right now?

As you already know, I name my recipes purposefully. Our recipe to address physical factors like pain is called Blow You Away (Twice) Brownies! We will prepare this together shortly.

Have I got your attention? Don't worry, it's just cooking, but it might get you "cooking."

But sometimes sexual frequency discrepancy is the product of emotional and relational problems. If one partner is suddenly less interested, avoidant, or making excuses, therapists ask, what's changed? Are there new stressors at home or work? Are there unequal burdens of childcare, household management, or financial responsibility? Are there other needs that aren't being communicated, let alone met?

Nothing kills an amorous mood quicker than anger or resentment. So, when she's saying "no," does it mean she doesn't want more sex or more sex with *him*?

Entire books have been written about the way that trust, similar values, respect, compassion, and honesty create intimacy and promote sexual desire, and how the absence of these components can harden a couple as quickly and solidly as cooling caramel. In fact, if you want the visual on that, here is a quick recipe that will illustrate how fast a "caramel" can harden. It's a cracker and caramel crunch—I call it: Caramel Couple in a Crunch Candies.

Nothing like the snap of hardened candy to simulate a rigid relationship. You might crack up when you get the metaphor of these Caramel Couple in a Crunch Candies. See Extra Recipes, Appendix B.

When we cook, we will most certainly be intimate and connected to what we're doing as well as to the person we're doing it with, and we'll highlight the way that translates to love and life.

In Cooking Therapy for sexual discrepancy aimed at emotional and relational issues, we think about recipes that have "ingredients" one partner may love while the other finds distasteful. First, you need to know if your partner doesn't like an ingredient or even a method of baking. In food terms, has your partner been eating your lemon chicken even though she can't stand citrus? Has he praised your famous fennel and breadcrumb pasta even though licorice makes him queasy? Communication is essential. Then, commitment and compromise follow.

Perhaps, then, that pasta can be made with basil not fennel, and maybe that chicken dish can be reworked as a lovely mango Cornish Hen!

Together we will make a recipe that addresses communication and compromise. You will have many opportunities to alter the amounts *and* the ingredients.

For our session, get ready to be clear, clever, and creative with tacos, aptly named: Tune-In and Talk to Me Tacos!

And then still, sometimes the solution to frequency discrepancy might also involve a *shift in perspective.* Some therapists believe one partner will always have higher desire than the other. If that's the case, it's important for both to rid themselves of any feelings of being flawed or wrong—in other words no guilt or shame or low self-esteem allowed, as we discussed at the beginning of the chapter.

Sometimes men and women can wonder if there's something wrong with them for wanting "so much," while their partners are wondering what's wrong with them for not wanting it more. This is despite loving the other partner without question. Just as you would accept you or your partner's love of exercise, travel, pets, or reading, why is it so outrageous to accept that *desire* may not be equivalent? I mean, you don't feel bad if you don't like watching CNN as much as he does and he doesn't care all that much for *Antiques Roadshow.* Some may require more sleep, more exercise, more mental stimulation, or physical exercise. Chances are you're bound to have different levels of interest in most things.

Even more, the levels of sexual desire in a marriage can change, or more accurately, ebb and flow, *and that's natural!* A little bit of acceptance of the changing tides of desire can go a long way toward reducing anger and confusion.

For example, if he doesn't want more sex, that doesn't mean she's not desirable. And if she's opting out, it's possible she'd pass on Brad Pitt too.

I have a friend, a woman in her fifties, who claims that she can feel five different temperatures in five minutes. One minute she's burning up, the next she wants to stand in front of the freezer naked or stick her head out of the car window like a Golden Retriever. These are physical feelings. But here's a lesson for you: Sexual desire can work the same way. Just because you're cool to the idea on Monday doesn't mean that Tuesday won't bring a hot surge.

We haven't covered all of the many reasons for frequency discrepancy but often therapists make concrete suggestions to reduce shame and arouse libido. After all, society signals early that men should like and want sex, while the messages for women change from age to stage. Sex therapists encourage clients to take charge of their arousal, suggesting that they notice the sensual stimuli in the world; the sexy billboard, a glance from that guy in the hardware store, a partner's touch.

Once you feel the feeling, then make a plan, whatever that plan entails, from a spa day to a sitter to a nap. It could be that you'll watch a sexy movie or read an erotic novel.

In our Cooking Therapy session, we will practice becoming aroused by sight, smell and touch. As Buddha instructed, we will give to the food and get much in return; we will give to the food and the food will give back.

Let's cook!

Taking Stock

I think taking stock of what's in your proverbial cabinet is always the first step to preparing a recipe. Cooking Therapy is "ripe" with metaphors and we'll be using quite a few going forward.

No doubt you have some ingredients at home (your past experiences and your partner's traits) and some you'll have to procure (a new way of thinking). If you are reading this, then you want to satisfy your partner and yourself and/or you're wondering about why one of you wants more sex than the other. Let's look at what's in your sexual and relationship pantry.

1. **Canned Goods** – these are the things that last forever! Take that same brand of pinto beans you've been using in your chili since 1996, and now ask yourself, are our routines ones that I want to use or discard? In other words, identify experiences that are enjoyable and you want to keep as well as some which are familiar but boring and you'd like to unload. Even more, could there be a can that you've never used, perhaps those artichoke hearts hiding in the back? No doubt with a little effort and creativity, they might satisfy.

2. **Ho Hum Dry Ingredients** — This means just what it says, like the cereal or rice. Is your "pantry" full of items from the same old shopping list you've used for years? Come on! Try to sub out the Corn Flakes and Uncle Ben's for some muesli and couscous. Upgrade your "goods" and think about a new spin on old favorites. And I do mean everywhere.

3. **The Cupboard is Bare** – perhaps it's been that long since you had any food in the pantry? Or even thoughts about food? Take a walk down the aisles of the supermarket and restock! You might actually want to practice thinking about…. ahem…food…for a change.

4. **Overstuffed Shelves** – If you're like many of us, your pantry looks like you've been preparing for the apocalypse. If your life is so full that you can't find yourselves or the time to be together anymore, it's time for a major spring cleaning. I would bet, however, that there's a great deal of good food in there just waiting for you to partake.

5. **Perfect Pantry** — Everything's there you need to make an excellent meal. Now you've just got to do it! That's exactly what Cooking Therapy is for; reminding yourself that you have everything you need to start. So let's do just that.

Food for Thought

One word we haven't really mentioned in this chapter is *relaxation*. I've never known anyone who could feel better in a frenzy. The same applies to every sexual situation we've explored. If you can relax both physically and spiritually, your body and your emotions just work better.

In cooking, there are moments when timing is critical. That's why I've specifically chosen recipes today that do *not* require quick action or moments of tense worry or guessing. Again, the difference between cooking and Cooking Therapy is focusing on the issue, noticing the process, enjoying and being present in the act. Wow, it already sounds a lot like sex.

Remember, Cooking Therapy is no substitute for Talk Therapy, and it's not a replacement for Couples Therapy. Rather, it's a tangible kind of therapy that can foster change in a different way, *because* it doesn't take place in the usual way, with therapist and client facing each other, making eye contact. Steve Jobs knew that "walking meetings" were always more productive than typical desk meetings, which could create a boundary between boss and employee that was more of a barrier to clear or creative decision making. Read more of his theory at *theladders.com*.

A 2016 study in the journal referenced above found that "although eye contact and verbal processing appear independent, people frequently avert their eyes from interlocutors during conversation. This suggests that there is interference between these processes." Basically, this means that it can be more difficult to process thoughts when you have to look someone in the eye under certain conditions.

As we proceed, obviously, you don't have to look me in the eye! All I ask is that you read the recipes first and follow the directions. In the case of Blow You Away Twice Brownies, you may split the two sessions into two. Why? Check out the first method and you'll soon understand why.

BLOW YOU AWAY (TWICE) BROWNIES

As I mentioned, this recipe comes from Estelle Groman Feldman, a wonderful mother and grandmother and butter/sugar creamer extraordinaire. Before I forget, I want to add that my mom always began the project by announcing that today she was on "a Big Brownie Mission!" My 13-year-old self, angry at being forced into slave labor (also known as assisting), and not yet a Sous Therapist, chose to rename the project as "my mom's Big BM." I thought it was funny. My mom, less so. As for anger and humor? There really is no place for the former in cooking or sex, but the latter is greatly underused in both!

INGREDIENTS
- 1 cup butter (2 sticks) softened, not melted
- 2 cups sugar
- 1 ½ cups flour, self-rising for recipe #2
- 1 cup walnuts (optional)
- 4 eggs

- 4 squares unsweetened chocolate, melted (4 ounces)
- 1 teaspoon vanilla

Remember, Cooking Therapy is mindful and purposeful. That's the difference between a therapy and an activity. You may think it's silly to make the same recipe twice in two different ways but I'm asking you to consider following my lead. Be mindful and conscious of every step so it sticks like flour and water and resonates in life.

Brownie Recipe #1, with some elbow grease, sometimes known as pain.

1. Preheat oven to 350 degrees. This means you are consciously getting ready to cook. Spontaneity doesn't work in heating the oven or in addressing an issue, but planning does.

2. Grease and flour two 8x8 pans (no baking blend spray). Remember when we didn't have spray? It wasn't easy to butter two pans and get all those nooks and crannies and it sure was messy to flour the pans. Although not exactly painful, you will find it arduous, and when sex or even cooking is too arduous, it, too, is difficult to enjoy.

3. Cream together butter and sugar till smooth. Okay, enough said. Take the back of the spoon and cream the butter and sugar together for a *long* time. If you've been working out it might not be so bad but probably takes a good 15-20 minutes and you will want to switch hands I suspect. Not fun.

4. Ice your sore arm. Just kidding. Kind of.

5. Melt chocolate in top of double broiler. No cheating. No microwave. This takes some time and attention, and is kind of a pain, especially to clean.

6. Add chocolate to mixture. Again, by hand. The point is, by now you're getting the idea that this rather simple recipe takes a lot of work. You may even be in a sweat.

7. Add eggs one at a time. You will have to do this in both recipes. Yes, there are some steps that can't be skipped in any activity.

8. Sift flour and gradually add to batter. Again, you are doing the stirring. If you haven't figured it out by now, we are going to be making *a stark* comparison about what sex (I mean brownies) may feel like now, and what it doesn't have to feel like.

COOK YOUR MARRIAGE HAPPY

9. So now just add the vanilla and nuts. Mix and mix and mix again, then spoon equal amounts of batter into each pan. Bake for 30 minutes, approximately.

10. Let cool and cut into squares. Are you exhausted? Feel free to take a shower or nap while the baked goods are cooling. Be thankful I'll let you use your dishwasher if you have one!

Yield: 32 brownies.

Brownie Recipe #2, same ingredients, but without pain.

1. Preheat the oven to 350 degrees.

2. Spray the two pans.

3. Combine softened butter (nuke to soft consistency if you need to) and sugar using paddle attachment in electric bowl stand (like a Kitchen Aid.) Keep mixer stirring on medium for duration.

4. Melt chocolate approximately 30 seconds in microwave and add to bowl.

5. Add eggs one at a time.

6. Sift self-rising flour and gradually add to bowl.

7. Add vanilla and nuts if using and add to mixture.

8. Bake for 30 minutes and let cool. Enjoy a hot cup of coffee. I suspect you're neither exhausted or depleted. In fact, you may outright feel like dancing!

Yield: 32 brownies.

Look, if you've followed the prescription and made each brownie recipe, one without any modern aids, you get the point. Many physical issues are no longer untreatable. Whether your batter is dry or limp, small or large, old or new, there are any number of contemporary fixes to turn the process from arduous to amorous.

Remember this: **lack of pain contributes to desire and better sex!**

So, see your doctor, your ob-gyn, your yogi, your therapist, the Internet, or simply share your physical concerns with your BFF. It's a start. Then never make Blow You Away Twice Brownies #1 again. And if you want, you can thank my mom. Just don't mention (ssh) s-e-x.

TUNE-IN AND TALK TO ME TACOS

Tune out the noise (and cell phone, iPad & Laptop) and tune-in to yourself or your loved ones with these "Talking Point" Tacos.

This is my own recipe. I originally created it to address the tentative child who is reluctant to try new things. I also wanted to satisfy a variety of tastes and keep the kids at the dinner table. I thought it would be hard to text and spin a Lazy Susan (turns out, not so much!). Thus, the "no phones at dinner" rule. If you happen to have kids and have the same rule, make sure you collect the phones and put them in another room. My friend Ronni swears her son can text on a phone in his pants pocket while looking her straight in the eye!

But back to the matter at hand. This recipe is also perfect for addressing an emotional or relationship problem. It's about communication and compromise. You can use a Lazy Susan or a series of small bowls. For the toppings, something between a ramekin and a coffee mug will do.

INGREDIENTS
- Any pre-packaged taco package that offers both hard and soft taco shells
- 1 pound of ground beef AND 1 lb of either chicken, or turkey
- 2 packages grated cheese of your choice
- 10 toppings of your choice*

*Some ideas are tomatoes, lettuce, onions, green and black olives, salsa, sour cream, scallions, guacamole, etc. Some people shave chocolate into their tacos to simulate a Mol'e sauce. The toppings are up to you but I want a full ten!

1. Take out two saucepans and put the beef in one and the poultry in the other. The idea here is to think about satisfying two people. If, however, you know for sure that you both like one or the other, making only one is fine. More on this later.

2. Sauté as per the box directions, splitting (if you have two proteins) and adding the taco seasoning. As you do, I want you to think quite consciously about the word seasoning. What does it do? It adds a particular flavor, spice and depth, no? And aren't those two ingredients necessary for any relationship?

3. Drain your protein and reserve. Look, so many culinary functions have metaphors for life, don't they? Think about reduction, concentration, caramelization, essence. But 'drain' can be super powerful! As the excess liquid goes out of the dish, remind yourself that you're willing to lose what dilutes your marriage, and reserve the best of everything.

4. Arrange the toppings in your Lazy Susan or in your bowls or mugs. Arrange them in a circle if possible to signify, like a circle, that your marriage cannot be broken. As per the package directions, heat up both hard and soft tacos. You are going to make a taco out of the one you like *most*! Stay with me here. Remember we talked about not communicating your needs and not building up resentment and frustration? Here is where you first make a taco exactly to your liking. This is *your* taco, exactly how you like it. You don't settle for the chicken because there's not enough beef.... you don't skimp on the ingredients you love for any reason. This is your taco. Go ahead, I'll wait! ... So delicious right? It feels good to get what you want. That's good selfishness. It makes you a contented and fulfilled person who isn't frustrated and wants others to be happy too. And by the way, content and happy people feel sexier and more intimate.

5. And now comes the compromise. You are going to make a second taco with the shell you like least. Yep, least. But don't panic, I'm not going to make you eat an entire taco of things you don't like. I'm going to ask you to add three things you wouldn't normally add but that your partner would. It's the honor system. Of course, it goes without saying that you should *never* add anything that you're allergic to, yes? It may go without saying but I'm saying it anyway! Don't do it! Okay, now as you eat the different but not life-threatening taco, I bet you'll be pleasantly surprised. Because compromise is almost never as bad as you think. And while this one is forced, it has what I call 'legs'. Let me explain.

In step five, we experienced a concrete example of satisfying our own needs. This should relate to all areas of your life. Food is just the messenger.

In step six, we experienced the sensation of enjoying someone else's tastes. Chances are that if you and your partner have grown apart sexually due to lack of communication or compromise in *other* areas of the marriage, that's exactly what's creating an intimacy void and contributing to frequency discrepancy.

Communication and compromise contribute to intimacy and better sex!

No doubt you will be making these tacos for more than yourselves. Do encourage your partner and even kids to join you in the purposeful acts of both fulfillment and compromise. No need to mention the sex part to the kids!

MASTERbakeTION: NO TRIFLING THING

Yes, once again, this recipe is purposefully and playfully named. I combined elements from several recipes for this session. We are going to make a trifle (also a name that invokes frivolity) with pudding, and the title is a play on self-fulfillment. Pudding is a highly underrated and truly sexy ingredient. Smooth, creamy, simple, yes, but it lingers on the tongue and takes hold, causing multiple......'mmmm's. Even alone, topped with a dollop of whipped cream, pure ecstasy.

Speaking of ecstasy, some of what we lose in a marriage that's sexually out-of-sync has to do with laziness in terms of igniting our own desire. Making a date for sex, buying some nice lingerie or oils, prepping the room, perhaps some visual aids, and even just anticipating and thinking about it during the day; all of these can be erotic and stimulating. I don't want you to be lazy about your own arousal, and for that reason we are making the pudding for the trifle from scratch, no instant!

This practically "orgasmic" recipe is called a trifle but is hugely sensual.

INGREDIENTS
For the pudding:
- ½ cup white sugar
- 3 tablespoons unsweetened cocoa powder
- ¼ cup cornstarch
- ⅛ teaspoon salt
- 2 tablespoons butter, room temperature
- 2 ¾ cups milk
- 1 teaspoon vanilla extract
- Shot of bourbon or amaretto* (optional)

For layering the trifle:

· 1 store bought pound or angel food cake cut into cubes
· 1 cup each exotic fruit like kiwi and mango

1. In a saucepan, stir together sugar, cocoa, cornstarch and salt. Place over medium heat, and stir in milk. Bring to a boil, and cook, stirring constantly, until mixture thickens enough to coat the back of a metal spoon. The stirring is the key here. Although this is a simple recipe, the stirring is so important that it's the difference between success and the garbage pail. Purposefully focus on what you are doing. By stirring or keeping things moving, you are not allowing the mixture to get clumpy or burned. Just like in a marriage, this dish requires your total attention for a short time. That is giving to the dish and being present in the act. You are also stirring up some of your own emotions! Go with it and have fun. As you run the spoon around the pot can you think about what makes you warm and fluid inside? And if you happen to feel stirrings from the stirrings? Hold that thought for later!

2. Remove from heat, and stir in the butter and vanilla. Stir in liquor if you're feeling naughty and that's naughty in a good way! Let cool briefly. Then chill in the refrigerator until ready to compose.

3. When chilled, stir a little pudding in the bottom of a trifle dish or large glass bowl.

4. Then layer cake, pudding, and fruit two to three times. As you're layering, and when the trifle is set, take a moment to think about the many layers involved and the way they *come together.* Think about the pudding and the textures it takes and how that mirrors the varied emotions in a relationship. You can start with something watery and diluted, with separate parts, and stir together a creation that's harmonious, thickened, both hot and cold, both soft and solid, both tantalizing and satisfying. Pudding. Marriage. So close.

Yield: Approximately 10 servings.

Clean Up (Process!)

Ultimately, bridging the desire gap may incorporate a medley of strategies; physical screening, emotional exploration of both partners' needs, sexual and otherwise, and a willingness to exercise both patience and action as needed. I hope our Cooking Therapy session will spark some sexual desire, but also the desire to talk about the options together, and whether you choose professional help, a mental shift, a trip to the drug store, or all of the above, eventually you might find yourselves on the same frequency about frequency.

Often in therapy, a therapist begins by helping the client prioritize issues, then contracting to set goals to address the most important ones. We're ahead of the game because we've already singled out one pressing issue. However, chances are that there are others; what we call co-occurring issues, and these may come up for you while participating in Cooking Therapy because anytime you focus on a problem you're uncovering new feelings, perhaps old hurts, certainly new perspectives; think of it as an excavation.

Today we looked at one component in your life, sexuality sync issues, and addressed three potential causes in a concrete way. You should feel clearer, more purposeful, and more hopeful that *you* have the power to address and improve your situation. I am so proud to be your Sous Therapist and of you for taking the time to try something new. You're worth it and your marriage is worth it.

Are you ready to try Cooking Therapy on your own? Keep reading.

COOKING THERAPY TAKEAWAY NOTES:

- Choose a recipe purposefully.
- Gather the ingredients your marriage needs.
- Prepare to follow new directions.
- Be thoughtful about the steps.
- Perform them mindfully.
- Expect slow change.
- Sit back, applaud your effort, and smile. You're quite the dish!

Cook Your Sexually-Out-of-Sync Marriage Happy on Your Own

By using the steps above and applying them to any recipe, you can practice Cooking Therapy on your own. You can incorporate it into any regular dinner or meal. However, in order for Cooking Therapy to truly be therapeutic, you should respect it as a legitimate therapeutic modality and engage in it as you would a session with your therapist.

First, no interruptions. That means no cooking with the family running in or out, no answering the phone, no texting, and no television. The power of the therapy is focus and concentration.

Second, make an appointment with yourself for the session. Preparation is important. You wouldn't go to a therapist's office without some research and planning so don't engage in Cooking Therapy haphazardly.

Commit. It's not okay to let your mind wander. Commit to using metaphor and analogy during every step of the process. For instance, during a session utilizing a Mixed Berry Pie we would take a few minutes to just stare at the freshly washed mélange of colorful berries. Don't cheat yourself by diluting the experience.

Here is a recipe you can try from *Allrecipes.com*. I call it: *Stop and Smell the Berries Pie. Pause. Smell. Notice. Appreciate. Everything you need (plus the ingredients) to try this at home. See Extra Recipes, Appendix B.*

Forgive failures. Every recipe you try, just like every strategy you employ, is not always going to work. Don't look at *any* finished product as a failure. The activity is enough. This is about cooking as process not food as result. There is no such thing as a failure. Pie becomes pudding, bread becomes crackers, meatloaf morphs into sloppy joes. Of course, if the dish comes out super badly, by all means, throw it out. You don't want your food, and yes, your relationship, to make you sick.

Thank you for the opportunity to come into your home and your kitchen. I wish you happy cooking, happy marriage, and happy you!

DB, *The Sous Therapist.*

Cook Your
Stale Marriage Happy

Every marriage goes through a natural ebb and flow. There are good times and bad, excitement and ennui, volatility and peace. The stale marriage has its own unique characteristics. Marital malaise occurs for a myriad of reasons and for most marriages at some time.

And that's understandable. So many milestones happen directly *to* us as individuals before marriage, so that even if your career is progressing and your kids keep making the honor roll, there is a natural lull once vows have been taken, often a kind of slower momentum as you settle into the next phase of life as a couple. And this can last for many months and years without us even realizing it! Why? Because we are busy with other things and the marriage may seem like something that doesn't require attention. You know, like those recipes that say, "marinate for three hours or let sit overnight if possible?" And you think, check! That dish is done!

But it's not really *done*, is it? Even after letting the chicken sit, you still have to take it out of the fridge, bring it to room temperature, uncover, and cook! See where I'm going with this? You may have the most solid marriage ever formed, the most savory of flavors, you may be best friends and soul mates, but you are not done.

A marriage can marinate but eventually it has to get cooked!

A marriage has so many benefits: companionship and an end to loneliness (*See note: lonely together!), financial advantages, a partner with whom to start a family and as biologists insist, the fulfillment that comes from connection, which is our human instinct. But that's the good news and bad. Spending so much time with another person requires skills; adaptation, diplomacy, compromise, communication, and flexibility to name a few.

In other words, in addition to the wonderful benefits of having a partner, you now also get to bicker with the same person over the same quirks (please just rinse the bowl when you put it in the sink!) or habits (arriving at 7:00 pm is truly *not* the same as 7:20!) over and over again. And you may be a whiz at ignoring or blocking out, but over time, ignoring can lead to disconnect and blocking out can create distance. And if you're tired of repeating yourself, you may tire of communicating at all. *This can not only lead to avoidance, but result in resentment, and yes, the dreaded lonely together.

Think about the last time you found a forgotten item at the back of the fridge. Was it fresh? Tasty? Bright? Did you want to eat it immediately? What about that beautiful artisanal baguette that went so well with last night's lasagna? If you left it on the counter, unattended, is it crispy and fresh or hard and stale? Now think about a marriage that's met the same fate! A marriage that's been forgotten, either to be wrapped, sealed, or placed in the foreground.... well, you get the picture.

But take heart!

A stale marriage is not a ruined marriage! It just needs a little attention!

Let's Take Stock

Your partner is one of the items you have at home!

When is the last time you took stock, and made a list of his or her ingredients (aka attributes)? Many couples feel that they have nothing left to cook with and chances are they're wrong. Here's an example. On the cooking site *Allrecipes.com* you can enter ingredients you have on hand as well as those you don't. One click and you have a list of recipes you can make. Try it with even the most unrelated and random items. I searched eggs, fruit, and chicken and actually got a recipe for Polenta Dressing. Who knew? Taking stock of your partner is no different. He or she has a shopping list of attributes, they are the ones you have to work with, and the ones you have on hand. There are sweet ingredients as well as salty, and maybe even some qualities that aren't always apparent for what they do, like butter, which can keep things from sticking or be the glue in a dish, or eggs, which can provide lightness.

So, take a moment, before we even cook, and make a list. I mean it. Get a pen or your phone and write it down. I'll wait!

List the ingredients in your partner that adds the following to the marriage:

- Sweetness
- Saltiness (a catalyst for rising)
- Smoothness (keeps from getting stuck)
- Lightness
- Hidden flavor
- Binding

Now, set the list aside and let's talk about amounts and what they do.

Sweetness is hard to overdo in a marriage and most likely that's not your problem or why you're reading this book. If your partner is too sweet, chances are you're simply missing one of the other ingredients for balance, so keep reading about amounts.

Salt, on the other hand, can be wonderful in baking, but in small doses. In tiny amounts, salt can give a marriage wit, energy, and laughter; for most delicious desserts salt adds just the right amount of assistance so that all of the other ingredients work at their peak. But too much salt can kill a dish. In Cooking Therapy, like in baking, we often work with precise amounts to give you a visual reminder. You have to make the leap and apply it to your marriage. Do you or your partner add too much salt? Most recipes call for "a pinch."

What does that look like in real life? A pinch is a joke here and there, not daily sarcasm. A pinch is gentle teasing, not habitual bickering. A pinch is a cranky moment, not a constant culture of negativity.

Smoothness is quite often desirable in cooking, but sometimes the recipe calls for a Julienne cut, a chunky homemade salsa, or for a batter to look like small peas. And isn't that a lot like life? Nobody has smooth sailing all the time and how would we appreciate those long smooth straightaways if not for the bumps in the road? So a few lumps are not a problem. But when the marriage feels like a rough chop more often than a creamy mousse, you both need to look at what's to blame. What (or who) is responsible for smoothing feelings, smoothing events, and generally creating calm? This is important information—if one of you is looking for a Cream of Wheat and the other is going for oatmeal, that's an imbalance that needs to be addressed.

Lightness is an ingredient every client I've ever met wants more of—in these days of political correctness, financial pressure, and uber demands on time, many of us have become terminally serious; the stress level for everyday folks is at an all-time high, as is anxiety and depression. No wonder your marriage may look and feel more like fruitcake than an angel food cake. To cook your stale marriage happy, you and your partner will have to shop for lightness, bring it home, and prepare it.

Hidden Flavor in a recipe is found in ingredients you may not want to eat by themselves. Spices like cumin, extracts like vanilla, and bits of lemon zest all add flavor and can "make the dish," but it's doubtful you'd sit down to a plate of zest and anyone who's ever tasted straight vanilla knows what I mean. So, what are your qualities, your spouse's, or even your marriage's unique hidden flavors? Have they been drying up on the shelf? Long out-lived their expiration date? Congealed into an unrecognizable paste? Try to remember. Every couple has charming quirks. One couple may have funny pet names for each other. Another used to take long walks every night after dinner. And still another may have liked eating Chinese food in bed! Whatever! Leaving out the hidden flavors dilutes and dishonors the dish.

Binding is an essential ingredient in every great recipe. A stew may use wine or butter, a bread uses flour, a salad takes dressing. Many marriages depend on kids to be the binding ingredient and while that's important, a marriage needs more. It needs something to help the couple stay connected as a couple – not as parents, not as coworkers, not as roommates, but as a couple. Think of the layers of a cake. Yes, the batter has flour (kids) and it has baking soda (budget) and it may have milk or applesauce (friends, family) but ultimately the layers are bound together and deliciously topped off by filling or frosting. If that cake has no frosting those layers are going stale by nightfall. If your marriage has been unfrosted for months or years… well, it's not too late to frost that cake!

Now you've made your list, you may already be starting to look at your partner in a new way (or the good old way). Joni Mitchell calls this "taking a new picture." And it's worth repeating that a stale marriage is not a ruined marriage. In the stale marriage, a couple of things may be going on. A little boredom is normal. Even savvy chefs get tired of the same recipe for Coq au Vin, no matter how magnificent the dish. Musicians drive you crazy when they reinvent the tune to your all-time favorite classic song during a concert, but it's understandable. No matter how much you liked the original *Layla*, Clapton needed a change! So, if by chance years later *you* still feel the way you felt the first time you met your mate or the first time the two of you were intimate, then you don't need guidance, you need to let the rest of us in on your secret.

Most couples report that when they were dating or newly married they showed their best selves, meaning, their most fun, adventurous, easygoing, and unencumbered selves. This isn't to say they were dishonest, just showcasing their best qualities. They were advertising, as in a press release. Once you live with someone and time goes by it's virtually impossible to sustain that level of energy and sunshine and you shouldn't feel pressured to do so. But as the perfect press release goes, so too can the romance and spontaneity. Ditto the communication. All of these may have to be "reconstituted" or reheated.

TIPS FOR KEEPING FOOD (AKA A COUPLE) FRESH

Vacuum seal the freshness into your marriage using these tips:

Remember to wrap tightly! By this I mean hug often.

Smell the milk carton. When was the last time you *really* asked your partner how things were going? And listened? Just like that milk, your loved ones go sour too—up to you find out what's going on. But please don't throw them out!

Cut off the hard parts! Ha-ha! Yes, every couple has flaws! Learn to look past or ignore the hard rind. Remember, your "mood" gets moldy now and then too!

TIPS FOR RAISING THE HEAT

Take your relationship from a tepid 225 degrees to a steamy 450 with these tips:

Preheat! Unless you're both 17, chances are you need to warm up the oven for best results. This can mean an hour of relaxation or foreplay, or…. a vacation!

Make time to savor the meal. Busy couples need to make time for "dinner." And dinner means everything from a meal to a morning. Call mom to watch the kids or call in sick to work. You're worth it.

Enjoy some old-time comfort food. Once upon a time you had goose bumps when you saw each other. Remember what it was about your "fried chicken" that made you happy.

Preoccupation with everything else in your life is another culprit. Some couples are so busy making "the side dishes" (i.e. the kids, job, friendships, or other family) that they forget to tune in to themselves as a couple; they forget to "stir, season, and bring to a boil." Or, like the chicken, they've simply let the marriage sit, uncooked for years. And that's where a therapeutic modality like Cooking Therapy can help. Cooking Therapy will help you to focus on your needs, your desires, and take the time to put them on the front burner for a change.

TIPS FOR FOCUSING ON THE MEAL AT HAND

Try these tips to savor your partner and not graze on the noise of the world.

Cook from scratch. This is a metaphor. In cooking, it means no cake mixes or prepared foods. In a relationship, it means no gadgets, no TV, no cell phones, no computer. Couples have a hard time with this. But I've seen miraculous results. Try talking to each other for a full hour about (here comes the dreaded F-word) your *Feelings*! About positive things. Sounds hokey but hokey couples are often the happiest. And they rarely fall into the category of lonely together. Give it a try.

Stir frequently. Busy lives don't have to preclude you from checking in with each other or being connected. Send a loving text or an emoji or a picture if you're apart. If you're both at home but busy there, a short shoulder squeeze or a grabbed hand in passing can keep the pot boiling and the pasta from sticking! So stir frequently for a smooth result. (Just a story to illustrate this further: When I worked as a school social worker we had students with attention deficits who utilized behavioral plans to stay focused and attentive. Often their desk was in the front of the room where there were less distractions. Additionally, the teacher would meander through the class and as she was talking let her hand come to rest on the shoulder of the child to "root" them in the present and keep them connected.) Think of "rooting" your partner, and yes, "rooting for them" so the two of you reap the same reward.

Let the dough rest. Busy couples often forget to breathe. The pressure of accomplishing tasks is often so great that the pot seems ready to blow the lid. Dial it back. Sometimes a slow flame makes the dish take longer but the depth and soul of the dish is almost always richer. You breathe. He breathes. You breathe. Rest and repeat. Watch your marriage rise.

Food for Thought

I'm not a big believer that every couple has a 50/50 responsibility for what's contributing to a stale marriage. Let's face it; some of us are more considerate, more communicative, and even more emotionally healthy than others; in other words, some of us are better relationship cooks. In a remote session of Cooking Therapy, I could never say who that is or comment on the odds of whether your marriage will thrive or not. What I can say is that you are here now, reading, searching, and hoping, and as I said earlier, the therapy has already begun.

In the next few pages you'll learn to use metaphor and methods to jump start and reheat the stale marriage. We'll be making three dishes together and you can try just one or all three. I'll also teach you how to do it yourself because with Cooking Therapy there is always something to be learned, each and every time. Cooking Therapy is not a cure all and is an excellent adjunct to traditional therapy. It's at once entertaining but purposeful and designed to address multiple issues or challenges in a totally different way. It's also the therapy I wholeheartedly urge and encourage you to try at home! Ready? Let's cook you up a new perspective and help you go from Stale to Spicy.

BREAK UP THE BOREDOM BREAD PUDDING

Today we'll be making Break Up the Boredom Bread Pudding. And that's what Break Up the Boredom Bread Pudding will do for you. You will never look at bread pudding the same way again. This recipe comes from Mark Bittman of the *New York Times*.

What I love about this recipe is its simplicity, which suggests its easier than you may think to tackle this project, its use of stale bread (duh) and also, because its part of an article entitled, "Turning Leftovers into Dessert!" How great is that?

INGREDIENTS

- ⅓ cup sugar
- Pinch salt
- ½ leftover loaf sweet egg bread like challah or brioche, cut into 2-inch cubes (about 5 to 6 cups)
- 2 eggs, beaten
- 2 cups milk
- 2 tablespoons (¼ stick) unsalted butter, more for greasing pan
- 1 teaspoon vanilla extract

Please make sure you've read the ingredients before we begin. Have you noticed all the "2"s? 2 cups milk, 2 tablespoons butter, 2 eggs...this is important. Cooking Therapy is about noticing everything! And a stale marriage is often one that's no longer noticed. This is a good time to ask: Do I notice my partner? Remember, Cooking Therapy is mindful and purposeful. That's the difference between a therapy and an activity. I want you to be mindful and conscious of every step and how it resonates in life.

1. Heat oven to 350 degrees. Your marriage is not a refrigerator or no bake cake! It needs you to turn it on.

2. In a small saucepan over low heat, warm milk, butter, vanilla, sugar and salt. Notice you can't just turn up the flame immediately. It's a slow process that requires some attention.

3. Continue cooking just until butter melts; cool. Again, this requires some thought. You don't want to over or underdo. And when you start changing your marital patterns you may have to step back after a few changes and let things cool down.

4. Meanwhile, butter a 4-6-cup baking dish and fill it with cubed bread. When you were slicing and dicing the bread, what did you think about? In Cooking Therapy, everything has meaning. Perhaps the cubes represent some parts of your marriage that are currently in pieces, but at the same time you can be hopeful that the pieces will come together again. Even buttering the dish should remind you that while we want the finished product to 'come together' we don't need to stick to the old ways.

5. Add eggs to cooled milk mixture and whisk. Now this is fun! Finally, you can use some energy to improve your marriage. Whisk away the

old and stale till they are merely memories! Adding fresh air to the mixture, your marriage, can only help.

6. Pour mixture over bread. As you pour think about how much you care that your marriage improves. Pouring itself is a healing act. Notice how your efforts are soaking into everything and binding the components.

7. Let soak for an hour. In the recipe, this is an optional step but I include it because I think everything improves in a relationship when changes are made slowly and people have time to 'soak in' those changes. For an illustration, google Systems Theory*. I have a very simple explanation below.

8. Bake for 30 to 45 minutes, or until custard is set but still a little wobbly and edges of bread have browned. I love this direction. A marriage isn't changed in a day. Like bread pudding, some parts have to set, some will still be wobbly and sometimes the edges remain a bit hard.

9. Serve warm or at room temperature. At the risk of being redundant, what could be better than taking a dish from cold to warm? By now you should be smiling.

Yield: Approximately 6 servings.

*Systems Theory suggests that when one person in a family system changes, then the entire system has to change to accommodate, and often that occurs stubbornly. Don't be disappointed if one session of Cooking Therapy initially produces opposition. Remember, you've been cooking the same dish the same way for a long time. Change is hard. Just because you're ready doesn't mean the system is—give it time.

NO MORE MONOTONY MEATLOAF

I've often said that re-heating a "leftover" marriage is like making a meatloaf; it's all in the seasoning. If only it were that simple.

But in many ways, making a savory meatloaf is a lot like taking a dish from plain to perky; a little spice, something to bind it all together, hands-on attention, and voilá, as long as you don't forget it, you should have something of substance in no time. In many ways marriage is nothing more than the sum of a bunch of pretty basic steps; it might not always be as easy as ground beef, bread crumbs, and egg, but it doesn't have to be Beef Wellington either.

Today we're going to make a sweet meatloaf because I want you to think about adding sweetness to your life. It's an applesauce meatloaf and its made in an 8x8 square pan shaped into a round. Like your wedding ring, a round is the symbol of things unbroken.

This recipe is an oldie but goodie (yes, you're thinking what I'm thinking-possibly like you) from the *Better Homes and Gardens New Cookbook*.

INGREDIENTS

Loaf:
- 1½ cups soft bread crumbs (2 slices)
- ½ cup finely chopped celery
- 2 tablespoons finely chopped onion
- 1 pound ground beef (or turkey)
- Salt and pepper, to taste
- 1 egg, beaten
- 1 teaspoon Dijon mustard

Topping:
- 1 tablespoon brown sugar
- ½ cup applesauce
- 1½ tsp vinegar (apple cider vinegar preferred)
- ½ teaspoon Dijon mustard

1. Once again, we need to preheat the oven to 350 degrees. And once again remind yourself that making changes, and in fact, heating anything, takes time and happens slowly. Notice that the recipe has two parts. One goes before and one goes after. Begin to think about how you were doing things before this day, and how you're going to do things differently, or "top it off' going forward.

2. Combine all ingredients that go into the loaf. When a recipe calls for combining several ingredients, the tendency is to short circuit your focus on each. Let's avoid that here. When beating the eggs think about them metaphorically for your communication skills, or the way you approach subjects. Do you beat them to death? Does that work? Do you under beat? Either way do they achieve the result you want? Beating takes patience, just as finely chopping the celery and the

onion does. Will you rush through or take your time? In this recipe, which calls for Dijon mustard and brown sugar, the amounts are important. Use the moment to ask yourself, what amounts of sweet or cynical do I put into my relationship. What about my partner? Sometimes Cooking Therapy is simply diagnostic and the basis for more work.

3.   Mix thoroughly. As all chefs know, there is just no other way to make meatloaf or meatballs without using your hands. Yep, you have to get in there and do the dirty work. It's messy and cold and sometimes downright disgusting. Yes, I am talking about marriage. Also, meatloaf. But remember, at the end you get something just dense enough, just soft enough, and hopefully delicious.

4.   Shape into a round loaf. There's really nothing more powerful than comparing your work at "shaping" a meatloaf to your work at shaping your part of a relationship. This loaf does not require perfection and neither do you. The recipe calls for shaping the mixture into a round loaf in a square pan. Just do your best.

5.   With a spoon, make a depression in the top of the loaf leaving about an inch around.

6.   Combine topping ingredients and pour into depression. Okay I really hate to use the word "depression" in an upbeat session of Cooking Therapy but we can 'mine' the metaphor to acknowledge that marital monotony can be depressing, and, if left untreated, can lead to more serious or clinical issues. So, when you make that depression please concentrate on the fact that you are *filling* it with something, and in this case, something sweet. Then bake the loaf for an hour, which will seal in the sweetness and your efforts.

Yield: 4 servings.

YOU ARE NOT AN ICEBOX CAKE

Smile. The message is clear. Although we're going to make a simple no-bake Icebox Cake or refrigerator roll, you are not cold, your marriage is not dead, and just because it doesn't bake every time doesn't mean it's not new, fresh, and delicious. Marriage is a marathon, and nobody is smoking hot every day, not even Beyoncé and JAY Z. This recipe appeared earlier as "Chill on it Icebox Cake," from Nabisco, but now we're going to use it in session. And I would love you to think of yourself as "chill."

INGREDIENTS
- 1 package (9 ounces) chocolate wafers
- 2 cups whipping cream
- 1 teaspoon vanilla

1. Beat whipping cream on high until stiff peaks form. There are so many sexual innuendos in that one instruction I think I'm going to simply leave you to it. Just remember, when you give your playful, active self to a task and to your marriage, you are more likely to get the same in return.

2. Gently stir in vanilla. Of course, your marriage requires your tender touch.

3. Spread 1 ½ teaspoons whipped cream onto each cracker. Stack. Take your time. The only labor in this recipe comes from being methodical at this moment for a short time.

4. Lay stack on side on platter and cover with whipped cream. This slightly delicate move should remind you of your creativity, commitment to the 'shape' of your marriage going from something forgotten and left to something formed with care.

5. Chill four hours or more. As always, while you want to be serious about attention to your marriage, you also want to chill. If one of you is always focused on what's wrong, that's, well…. uncool, to carry the metaphor. Years ago, I worked with some very anxious teens. I would ask them to write their problems on Post-It notes that we would put on the inside of the fridge and freezer to remind them to "chill" on some of their self-proclaimed "catastrophes," which were, indeed, very real to them. You are Not an Icebox Cake gives you permission to do the same.

Yield: 14 servings.

Clean-Up (Process!)

As you have heard me say before, often a therapist begins by helping the client prioritize issues, then write a contract to set goals that address the most important ones. We're ahead of the game because we've already singled out one pressing issue. However, chances are that there are others; what we call co-occurring issues, and these may come up for you while participating in Cooking Therapy because anytime you focus on a problem you're uncovering new feelings, perhaps old hurts, certainly new perspectives. Think of it as an excavation.

Today we looked at one component that may be part of your life – marital malaise, and we addressed it in a concrete way. You should feel clearer, more purposeful and more hopeful that you have the power to address and improve your situation. I am so proud to have been your Sous Therapist and of you for taking the time to try something new. You're worth it and your marriage is worth it.

Are you ready to try Cooking Therapy on your own? Keep reading.

COOKING THERAPY TAKEAWAY NOTES:

- Choose a recipe purposefully.
- Gather the ingredients that your marriage needs.
- Prepare to follow new directions.
- Be thoughtful about the steps.
- Perform them mindfully.
- Expect slow change.
- Sit back, applaud your effort, and smile. You're quite the dish!

Cook Your Stale Marriage Happy on Your Own

By using the steps above and applying them to any recipe, you can practice Cooking Therapy on your own. You can incorporate it into any regular dinner or meal. However, for Cooking Therapy to truly be therapeutic, you should respect it as a legitimate therapeutic modality and engage in it as you would a session with your therapist.

First, no interruptions. That means no cooking with the family running in or out, no answering the phone, no texting, and no television. The power of the therapy is focus and concentration.

Second, make an appointment with yourself for the session. Preparation is important. You wouldn't go to a therapist's office without some research and planning so don't engage in Cooking Therapy haphazardly.

Commit. It's not okay to let your mind wander. Commit to using metaphor and analogy during every step of the process. For instance, I use one recipe for a Berry Trifle *(see Extra Recipes Appendix B)* that involves a few minutes of just staring at the freshly washed mélange of colorful berries. Don't cheat yourself by diluting the experience.

Forgive failures. Every recipe you try, just like every strategy you employ, is not always going to work. Don't look at ANY finished product as a failure. The activity is enough. This is about Cooking as process not food as result. There is no such thing as a failure. Pie becomes pudding, bread becomes crackers, meatloaf morphs into sloppy joes. Of course, if the dish comes out super badly, by all means, throw it out. You don't want your food, and yes, your relationship, to make you sick.

Thank you for the opportunity to come into your home and your kitchen. I wish you happy cooking, happy marriage, and happy you.

DB, The Sous Therapist.

COOK
YOURSELF
HAPPY®

Cook Your Maybe-I-Made-a-Mistake Marriage Happy

Of all the life transitions you will face, sharing your life with another person may be the most challenging. While it's hoped that it will also be the most rewarding (eventually!) you will be called on to grow in ways you never knew or expected. Suddenly, your space, both physically and emotionally, is no longer just your own and your habits, thoughts, routines, values, and plans are to be shared.

You are no longer chairman of the board; you are co-founder of the company called:

The Two of You.

And while you may love this person with all your heart and soul, *adjusting to The Two of You can be a challenge.*

The two of you decide where to live, what to do, how to order your days, nights, and weekends.

The two of you decide what to eat and where, where to shop and what to buy.

The two of you decide who will be your friends and how to incorporate your families into your lives.

The two of you make financial decisions, entertainment decisions, lifestyle decisions, and truly big decisions about the family you're going to create *together.*

And you only have half a vote.

Then, there are the things you knew and love about each other but may have loved twice a week – not twice a day. That funny noise he makes when he eats, or her habit of clearing the plates the moment you finish, quickly goes from charming to annoying when it happens three times a day every day.

Add to that the things you didn't know! Some of these may be minor quirks that are easily worked out—toe clippings on the floor and not sealing the cold cuts aren't usually deal breakers in a marriage.

Slightly more difficult are tangible behaviors that have an emotional effect. He rarely helps with cleaning up or she spends every minute on her phone. These are behaviors that can have a negative effect on the partner, making them feel resentful or unappreciated. These are couple issues that are important and will take some illuminating and a willingness to hear and change. But they are also manageable if both parties are invested in a happy union.

But if you're continually shocked by behaviors that make you angry, sad, or cringe, then you're charged with shining a bright light on why you got married and what you can or want to do about it.

If you are at the point where you're wondering if the marriage was a mistake, you will have to get honest with yourself about these things and take a hard look at yourself in the process.

That said, every new marriage has a learning curve!

Let's begin to think about it like a recipe. A marriage is about the most complicated recipe you could ever endeavor to prepare; it's the cover of *Gourmet Magazine* or signature dish at the fanciest restaurant in town. For sheer difficulty and detail, it's the legendary Coconut Cake at the Peninsula Grill in Charleston. Yep, it's the hardest, most layered, and most ambitious recipe you've ever attempted! But you can do it. Just maybe not in an hour, or at first, without a willingness to learn and some work, right?

Every accomplished baker has thrown out numerous crusts before he or she got it just right. What kept them going through sticky dough and crumbling crust? Determination and education. They had to commit to working at it (yes over and over again) and they had to learn from their mistakes.

Your new marriage is no different, whether it's six months or six years new and even if it's a second or third marriage. Each marriage comes with its own set of specific hurdles; there may be children from a former spouse as well as the former spouse themselves! Was there a divorce, a death, and was the separating amicable or contentious? All of these come into play in a second marriage. On the other hand, a first marriage has very little context for compromise and negotiation. Plus, both of you may be very young or at least inexperienced.

So, either way, get ready to roll up your sleeves, lift your chin and prepare to work. We *will* make multi-step recipes *and* that Coconut Cake. Because marriage is complicated. But we'll also make a super easy salad that will employ the same strategies and impress upon you the same skills needed to examine, adjust, and evaluate your newer marriage. Ready? Let's crush this!

The Little Things

- He doesn't cover his mouth when he sneezes.
- She buys me things I can't use and don't want.
- He's always late.
- She's always early.
- He's a vegan.
- She loves a rare steak.
- Her laugh is kind of irritating.
- His laugh is too loud.

You get the picture. The list of complaints like these is often endless in a new marriage. They are not deal breakers. They are the little quirks and blips that highlight the difference between living *with* someone rather than with just yourself. If you notice, there are no philosophical differences here, but instead, habits, and habits can be tweaked if not outright unlearned.

Remember, quirks are not deal breakers!

In cooking the new marriage happy we'll spend a lot of time focusing on how to change or accept habits, because at the end of the day, you'll pick and choose what really matters, just as you would in a recipe. Let's start with that famous Coconut Cake. We're going to make it together and highlight the way it mirrors your marriage. There are several steps that are labor-intensive, just as it may feel to you to address the differences between you and your partner. Here's an example from my list:

He doesn't cover his mouth when he sneezes. Yuck, you find it disgusting. But you don't find him disgusting, right? Just this behavior. So even though you want to say "Ugh, cover your mouth that's gross!" you don't! Why? Not because you're wrong but because he will hear that you think he's disgusting and feel awful. The words won't "go down" easy. Instead, you say in your best loving voice, "Honey, would you mind covering your mouth when you sneeze so you don't spread germs and we can both stay free from colds? Thanks, honey, love you."

This might seem basic, but you'd be surprised how much blurting out of insensitive comments occur in the new marriage. That's the adjustment and the fear talking. You'll see that the very first step in the Coconut Cake is kind of like that. The recipe calls for corn starch, but you can't just put the corn starch in because it will clump. You have to "temper it" with water in order to make it "easier to blend in." And cumulatively, in both the cake and your relationship, these kinds of thoughtful decisions will make the difference.

Now that you see what I mean, let's get started. Please read through the recipe in its entirety and note there is an *overnight* component. This is purposeful. Your new marriage with the most minor quirks has less cemented and entrenched resentments and if treated intensely at the beginning can have everlasting effects. Don't cheat yourself of the chance to make big changes early on!

Although this is the original coconut cake from The Peninsula Grill, I've renamed it, as I always do, for our therapy session, because words are so powerful and will cement the lesson we'll learn. Our recipe is now, Neither Cuckoo, Nor Coco*nuts*, Cake.

NEITHER CUCKOO, NOR COCONUTS, CAKE

INGREDIENTS

Filling:
- 2 tablespoons cornstarch
- ½ cup sugar
- ½ cup unsalted butter
- 2 ¼ cups sweetened flaked coconut
- ¼ cup sour cream
- 2 tablespoons water
- 1 teaspoon vanilla extract
- 1 ¼ cups heavy cream

Cake:
- 3 ½ cups all-purpose flour
- 1 tablespoon baking powder
- ½ teaspoon salt
- 2 ¼ cups sugar
- 1 ½ cups unsalted butter, room temperature
- 5 large eggs
- 1 ⅓ cups heavy cream
- 1 tablespoon vanilla extract

Frosting:
- 2 (8 ounce) packages cream cheese, room temperature
- ½ cup unsalted butter, room temperature
- 2 cups powdered sugar
- 4 cups sweetened flaked coconut, toasted
- 1 teaspoon vanilla extract

Filling:

1. Stir cornstarch, 2 tablespoons water, and vanilla in small bowl to dissolve cornstarch. As you remember, we spoke about how to change habits in a way your partner can hear. Just like this first step, think too, about the word "dissolve." It's a big one. You have the power to "dissolve" tension or to let your exchanges "dissolve" into anger.

2. Bring cream, sugar, and butter to boil in heavy medium saucepan. This takes a bit of patience, right? Remember number two on the quirks list? Someone is buying gifts that the other person really doesn't want. Hmmm, instead of focusing on what the gifts are, how about the sentiment behind them? Someone is buying things for you they think will make you happy! Chances are a year ago that wasn't happening. Chances are you'd never boil up a bowl of cream, sugar, and butter, either, but at the end of the day you're going to have cake. And a person who thinks of the other person and gets them trinkets to say so? Kind of like getting cake.

3. Add cornstarch mixture and bring to boil.

4. Remove from heat and stir in coconut.

5. Cool completely. I can't stress these steps enough. Maybe your parents said it: never go to sleep on a fight. I promise you that if you don't react too quickly, your relationship will always go better. Just like this filling. If it went into a cake now it would run and seep out, accomplishing nothing. So, mix in the sour cream (a little patience and thought) and chill.

6. Mix in sour cream.

7. Cover and refrigerate overnight.

Cake:

1. Preheat oven to 325 degrees.

2. Butter and flour 3 9-inch round cake pans. Let's talk about the number 3. This is quite the layer cake, right? Well your marriage is made up of many layers, too. And trust me, three is not all that many! For now, it's the two of you and the newness, but later, and as you grow together you'll encounter layers that will test you. Remember this time, this simpler time, when it was *only* three layers!

3. Whisk flour, baking powder, and salt in large bowl to blend.

4. Using electric mixer, beat sugar and butter in another large bowl to blend. These two steps give you an opportunity to think about difference and blending. One bowl has the dry ingredients, another the butter blend. Separate pieces that will fold into each other to form something better.

5. Add eggs one at a time, beating well after each addition. For each egg, go back to the list in your mind. Can you deal with loud laughter? Funny sneeze? Tofu ice cream? I bet you can.

6. Beat in cream and vanilla.

7. Stir flour mixture into butter mixture.

8. Divide batter equally among pans. Dividing the batter into equal pans should promote a sense of organization and balance. You can and should want to each be equally present in the relationship. Three pans, three representations; you, your partner, the marriage. Because the marriage is a living breathing soul that needs to be nurtured.

9. Bake until tester inserted into center of cakes comes out clean, about 35 minutes.

10. Cool completely. This is a good time to talk about late vs. early, technically a minor difference but one of those that can *become* a real problem. Just as we wouldn't take the cake out early, you will have to negotiate time preferences with your partner. You may be a person who wishes that cake would be ready after only 25 minutes, but that just won't work. He may prefer if it stayed in for 45 minutes, but that doesn't work either. In a perfect world, you'd have a talk with your mate and you'd meet in the middle and it would all work out, but we know it doesn't usually end up that way. People have their own inner clocks. So, you may have to get creative the way a baker might. For instance, bakers use the freezer or an ice bath to accelerate cooling. Perhaps you have to tell your partner the reservation is for 7:00 pm when it's really 7:30. Or perhaps you need to set *your* watch ahead. Or his! This is not avoiding a solution, its self-preservation! Just ask anyone who's crossed the hump of the new marriage. Sometimes you just have to do what works.

Frosting:

1. Using electric mixer, beat cream cheese and butter in large bowl to blend. Remember how we talked about something like laughter? Hers may be too irritating, his too loud? Here we need that annoying loud beater to get to the delicious frosting. If you look at it that way, perhaps it's somewhat less annoying and more something to be embraced. Maybe you could try that with your partner, you know, the one over there you love and adore? ☺

2. Beat in powdered sugar and vanilla extract.

3. Place one cake layer on cake plate.

4. Top with half of filling.

5. Place second cake layer atop filling.

6. Top with remaining filling.

7. Place third cake layer atop filling.

8. Spread frosting over top and sides of cake.

9. Pat toasted coconut over top and sides of cake, pressing gently to adhere. Can be prepared up to one day ahead. Cover and refrigerate. Let stand at room temperature 3 hours before serving.

Yield: 12 servings.

All of these assembling and finishing tasks are the proverbial icing on the cake. The point of the frosting is to bind everything together into a beautiful and tasty treat. So, take the metaphors and apply it to your relationship. There are a lot of individual parts to a cake and you may not *love* every one of them but chances are with some attention and TLC, no matter what, you can end up with a damn fine cake. You may have coconut and prefer peaches. You may have buttercream and prefer cream cheese. Initially, you may even have a bunch of failed attempts at cake that end up as pudding. But hey, pudding's not so bad, especially if you dig in with two spoons. The lesson to takeaway is that you can have differences. If they aren't differences that are intensely *fighting* each other all the time, you will have your own signature and delicious dessert. It won't be CUCKOO or NUTS; it will be yours.

The Middle Things

So now we get to that next layer of problematic concerns that have you questioning whether the relationship works. These kinds of things might be tangible and/or beginning to affect the spirit:

- I don't like his/her friends.
- His/her family is difficult.
- Someone is working much more than imagined.
- He or she is always on the phone, iPad, etc.
- Our interests are not as in sync as I thought.
- I feel critical or criticized.
- Feelings of resentment or frustration are starting to build around communication.
- Someone doesn't feel heard.

Just as I promised, we're going to make a fancy recipe, this one is from the cover of *Bon Appétit*. Challenging? Less than you might think. Especially since the January 2016 cover is based on a cover that says "healthy-*ish*." How lucky is that and how coincidentally does that sound like where you are? Let me let you in on a little secret; most marriages are healthy-ish. It's not a failure, it's a goal. I'm always suspicious of those "perfect marriages" I hear tell of (urban legend?) and begin to wonder if the partners are more perfect or have perfected détente. More on that later. Because an unengaged marriage, while possibly uneventful, has nowhere near the joy of an engaged "'ish" team.

The *Bon Appétit* cover highlights the use of Chinese cookware called *Donabe*, which is a traditional tool for cooking rice. But no worries, you need no special equipment. We're going to make the Ginger Chicken Rice using the principles of a *Donabe* life, even if you don't have a *Donabe* (see the metaphors beginning to emerge) or even a rice cooker. And we're going to change our recipe's name from A Donabe life, to A Doable Life. So close phonetically, I couldn't resist. And the message again is this; both the dish and your marriage don't have to be perfectly healthy, don't have to have some magazine version of who you should be and what you should do. All you really need is to customize it so it works for you. When we begin, you'll note that the first instruction is always the same: One part rice, water is twice. Your relationship is the rice, and two parts water are the two of you.

A healthy-ish relationship can be healthy enough.

But first, let's talk about some of these deeper concerns. Ultimately, just like in a recipe, you have to customize your tolerance like your ingredients. And you may need to change how *you usually* do things. This is a good time to remind you that Couples Therapy is wonderful for teasing out the patterns and communication styles of each individual so that they are clearer about their wants and needs. Adding Cooking Therapy to an overall excavation of the relationship is a helpful adjunct and tangible visual tool.

Here's an example: One person likes to bake their muffins with sour cream and another uses applesauce. It's fair to say that most people have one or two things they will *never* eat. For me, it's black licorice. If I smell black licorice, I get nauseated.

Also, not crazy about butterscotch or root beer or nutmeg. If I had to eat these things every day or even several times a week, I'm pretty sure I'd be unhappy. Luckily, I don't have to eat them at all. I have a choice, so I don't.

In a relationship, some characteristics might not be your favorite, but might not be your black licorice either. For instance, while I will *never* drink root beer, you can disguise some butterscotch or nutmeg in ways I won't notice or at least mind much. As an example, chances are your partner's family is not going away anytime soon. Can you find a way to make them nutmeg?

Here is a quick story about how I turned traditional mac and cheese from *thepudgefactor.com* into a new recipe that's renamed as: "Plan to Make It Work Mac and Cheese."

There is no need to engage in a Cooking Therapy session with this recipe because the point is simple. The recipe called for one full tablespoon of dry mustard – let's think of that spoonful as the difficult family or annoying friends who would seem to have an extremely pungent impact on a dish that uses only two cups of elbow pasta. But, the beauty of the combination of ingredients is that the strong taste of mustard absolutely disappears into the milk and cheese. Trust me, I have a dear family member who hates mustard and loved this mac and cheese. She might well be horrified to learn it's in the dish! As long as we keep this between us, she'll never know! And just as with the mustard, your partner's "strong and pungent" family may well blend into the background if you create a mix that absorbs the heat. Alternately, I've occasionally used less dry mustard or substituted a little regular mustard (meaning not *all* the family has to be together *all* the time, do they?) and the result was just as good.

The fact that the recipe freezes well has a message too. This mac and cheese is made in muffin cups. That means you can take them out one at a time, or a few at a time, instead of all at once. You see where I'm going with this, right? Of course you do. Same thing with the friends. *To plan to make Plan to Make It Work Mac and Cheese, see Extra Recipes, Appendix B.*

Here is another way to create the same tolerance for friends who "rub you the wrong way." Yes, of course we're doing a rub! It's the perfect way to illustrate how to minimize the flavors you don't like (see them less frequently) and add in some of the ones you do (your own friends!). *See There's the Rub in Extra Recipes, Appendix B.*

You can mix and match almost all of the spices in this rub to highlight or eliminate flavors. Cool it on the curry powder (his friend who undresses you with his eyes) or up the amount of garlic (his buddy from the office who is so smart). Can you take a little chili powder (her girlfriend with the annoying voice) but just can't stand ginger (her show-off colleague who brags about her money)? The point is, just like in a rub, you can choose the amounts, at least, without totally leaving out all of the components.

So remember, when it comes to family and friends, either you can see them less, incorporate others into the friend "mix" to dilute the tastes and aromas, or possibly have nights out alone when one partner has a root beer orgy and the other is happily out or at home with their own version of comfort food. Remember, too, you can do all three.

However, if you're not feeling heard, or worse, you're feeling devalued, kind of like *you're* the black licorice, it's time to open the pantry, take out the flavors you hate, and make room for more pleasant items. It's *never* okay to feel hated. But it's possible your partner doesn't even know how you feel. I once knew a couple who had Chinese food every Sunday night for years and then in a fit of rage the wife blew up one night and screamed, "And by the way I hate Chinese food!" Can you imagine if the first time they had that meal she had shared that it wasn't her favorite, rather than submit to what became a ritual of distaste and her perceived martyrdom? By the way, compromise is not martyrdom. Doing something nice for someone selflessly is much different than doing it while resenting it. Stop accepting hurtful criticism, stop eating Chinese food. Tell your partner what you like and want. It may not go down easy at first but in the long run your needs will be on the table. And if both of you are communicating in this rational, safe, and healthy way, chances are that all or most of your "meals" (aka issues) can be addressed in the "middle things" and before they become the "big things." And remember:

Compromise is healthy. Martyrdom? Not so much!

The recipe will help to crystallize theses skills so let's begin!

A DOABLE LIFE GINGER CHICKEN RICE

INGREDIENTS
- 8 ounces chicken thigh (boneless and skinless), cut into small cubes
- 2 rice-cups short grain rice, rinsed and drained, 1 rice cup is ¾ cup.
- 1 ounce peeled ginger, sliced into needle thin (1" long)
- 1 scallion, thinly-sliced crosswise
- Toasted white sesame seeds (to taste)
- 1 teaspoon sesame oil
- 1 ¼ cups dashi stock (can be substituted with chicken stock or vegetable stock)
- 2 tablespoons sake
- 1 ½ tablespoons usukuchi shoyu (light-color soy sauce) or regular soy sauce
- ½ tablespoons nampla (fish sauce; can be substituted with soy sauce)

1. In a bowl, combine the chicken, sake, soy sauce, and fish sauce. Mix well by hand.

2. Cover tightly with plastic and let the chicken marinade for 30 minutes. It's important to stop and think about "combining." You've mingled many things in the first few months or years of your relationship; hard goods and soft. As you add each ingredient think about all the things you've blended together. And most important, *use your hands.* Your 'hands' have been in this, you didn't just walk, in a daze, into your life. Take ownership of the purposeful acts you've performed.

3. Meanwhile, in the rice cooker or if you are using, in the "Kamado-san,"* combine the rice, dash stock, and sesame oil. Let the rice soak for 20-30 minutes. I like to think about soaking when it comes to a new relationship. Sometimes your recipe has to rest or settle or congeal to come out right. Don't be so manic about fixing that you don't give the relationship time to settle into itself.

4. Spread the ginger over the rice. Add the chicken with the marinade liquid and spread on the top. This should make you think of all the good you're creating. We haven't even touched on the benefits of being with someone, sharing your life, and giving and receiving emotional support. Enjoy not being alone and coming together.

5. Cover cooker and cook over medium-high heat for 13-15 minutes, or until 2-3 minutes after the steam starts puffing out of the top lid. If you want the nice crust ("okoge") on the bottom cook for extra 1-2 minutes.

6. Turn off the heat and let rest for 20-30 minutes. Once again, Rome wasn't built in a day. If someone works too much or is too "connected" to technology as so many are today, think about scripting real 'resting' moments into the day. Cell-free dinners and Tuesday night 'don't be late' date nights are as tangible as stirring, spicing, and covering the pot.

7. Uncover and fluff the rice. Garnish with some scallion and sesame seeds. No one needs to tell you that with tenderness, patience, attention and gentle blending, the marriage gets fluffier and the problems become lighter. It's possible, attainable and yes, *doable*!

*This recipe calls for a Kamado-san or special rice cooker with a double lid. If you have one, great. As already discussed, however, there is no need. A heavy medium pot will do just fine. And if you customize this recipe, remember always that while one of you may begin this session of Cooking Therapy, it will always take "two cups" of water, to make "one cup" of your rice, turn out well.

Yield: 4-5 servings.

The Big Things

If you've read this far, then by now you are feeling one of two things. One, you may feel relieved because your problems feel like they fit into the first two groups, the little and medium things. Or, you may be even more concerned because we haven't even touched the level of concern or explored the issues you feel you're facing. Take heart, just because you feel like there are big things in your way, it doesn't mean that your marriage will fail. You just have to shine a slightly stronger light on what's going on and be willing to do some work that may seem arduous, tedious, and maybe even a bit stilted. That's okay, you're worth it.

Some big concerns might be:

- I don't feel attracted to my partner.
- I disagree constantly with his views.
- I find myself inwardly cringing or rolling my eyes when he…
- Our values are different about money and children.

So of course a natural question will be, where were you and what were you thinking when you made the decision to be with this person? Many people get married or enter into a relationship for all of the wrong reasons. Were you afraid of being alone? Escaping something else? Looking to be saved? Settling? Without asking yourself the hard questions you won't have a good history to work from.

Believe it or not, some of the best recipes are more delicious because of their history. For example, your grandmother's baked ziti, or a dish created while the slaves left Egypt. *For your own walk down memory lane, try Grandma's Baked Ziti (also told to me by Donna Selman) and Nanny's Matzah Brei, see Extra Recipes, Appendix B.*

Trust me, if you look at where you are in context, and even if it doesn't fit the Brady Bunch school of decision-making, you're more likely to have the skills to evolve and have a healthy relationship.

So, no guilt, recrimination or regret, just honesty.

As always, remember that talk therapy is a layered and therapeutic standard for getting to the root of many "why's" in your life. Cooking Therapy will offer a different and experiential method to help you reframe and imprint a healthy evaluation and process. Let's begin.

Our recipe today will be a chopped salad. I can almost hear you asking, "a what?" A salad for my deep and major problems? Again, trust me, a salad is much more labor-intensive than many entrées I've prepared. And this one will test you!

MAKE-PEACE-NOT-WAR ISRAELI CHOPPED SALAD

I thought a recipe that channeled "in name" one of the most troubled regions on the planet was appropriate here. This is not meant to be a political statement, only to say that every conflict requires two parties to find acceptable terms. You will be the judge of whether or not the discord can be managed. There will be chopping. Lots of it. Because we are putting together a dish with lots of little parts, but they all have to come together in more or less equal and valued ways.

This recipe has been customized from *Saveur* magazine. As a side note, "saveur" in French means to savor or taste, but even more, to identify the flavor on the palate. For our purposes, this is a very present part of the process you are about to begin. Pay close attention to how you feel when you are chopping these bits and bites. Do you find it annoying or soothing? Painful or predictable? Much of what you "transmit" or identify about the process will inform your perception of how badly you may want or feel able to give to the marriage. Because one thing is for certain, many marital days are simply about chopping up life's little bits and putting them together in an eatable dish.

I'm not going to give you any more instructions than that. The directions and amounts are clear. Let the chopping, processing, and assembling begin. We'll talk after.

Many marital days are simply about chopping up life's little bits and putting them together in an eatable dish.

INGREDIENTS

- ¼ cup minced cilantro
- ¼ cup minced mint
- ¼ cup minced parsley
- 2 teaspoons ground sumac
- 1 teaspoons ground cinnamon
- 6 scallions, thinly sliced
- 4 cloves garlic
- 4 medium ripe tomatoes, cored, seeded, and minced
- 3 medium cucumbers, seeded and minced
- 2 serrano chilies, stemmed, seeded, and minced
- 1 red bell pepper, stemmed, seeded, and minced
- 1 large white onion, minced
- Kosher salt and freshly ground black pepper, to taste
- ½ cup olive oil
- Juice and zest of 3 lemons

Mix all the ingredients in a bowl. Let sit 20 minutes before serving.
Yield: Approximately 5 servings.

Well, how'd it go? Did you feel purposeful and productive? Many people report that the worst thing about struggling in a relationship is a sense of not being able to do something. I've chosen a recipe for you that is highly structured and directive and combats that, as no doubt you now well know. There is much to do in this recipe just like your relationship.

Alternately, did it feel endless and impossible and not worth it? You will have to explore that and make the connection. This is not to say that making a salad and your feelings around it are a prescription to keep or discard a marriage; but it is information.

With some clarity about your willingness to work at repairing the broken parts of your marriage, you're better equipped to identify your feelings and communicate your thoughts. If you have real concerns about 'the big things' after this exercise I highly encourage you to bring this up with the qualified individual or couple's therapist of your choice. And while you can improve understanding of every marriage through Cooking Therapy, you can't cook every one happy. Sometimes we just get to cook your marriage clearer. I hope that's been the case for you in this session.

Clean Up (Process!)

Once again, often in therapy a therapist begins by helping the client prioritize issues, then contracting to set goals to address the most important ones. We're ahead of the game because we've already singled out one pressing issue. However, chances are that there are others; what we call co-occurring issues, and these may come up for you while participating in Cooking Therapy, because anytime you focus on a problem you're uncovering new feelings, perhaps old hurts, certainly new perspectives, think of it as an excavation.

Today we looked at one component in your life, a feeling that you may have made a mistake, and we addressed three levels of concern. Only you can tell if you are ready to do the work to improve any of the areas where you think you may fall. But you should at least feel clearer, more purposeful, and more hopeful that you do have the power to address and improve your situation. I am so proud to be your Sous Therapist and of you for taking the time to try something new. You're worth it and your marriage is worth it.

Are you ready to try Cooking Therapy on your own? Keep reading.

COOKING THERAPY TAKEAWAY NOTES:

- Choose a recipe purposefully.
- Gather the ingredients your marriage needs.
- Prepare to follow new directions.
- Be thoughtful about the steps.
- Perform them mindfully.
- Expect slow change.
- Sit back, applaud your effort, and smile. You're quite the dish!

COOK
YOURSELF
HAPPY®

Cook Your Maybe-I-Made-a-Mistake Marriage Happy on Your Own

By using the steps above and applying them to any recipe, you can practice Cooking Therapy on your own. You can incorporate it into any regular dinner or meal. However, in order for Cooking Therapy to truly be therapeutic, you should respect it as a legitimate therapeutic modality and engage in it as you would a session with your therapist.

First, no interruptions. That means no cooking with the family running in or out, no answering the phone, no texting and no television. The power of the therapy is focus and concentration.

Second, make an appointment with yourself for the session. Preparation is important. You wouldn't go to a therapist's office without some research and planning, so don't engage in Cooking Therapy haphazardly.

Commit. It's not okay to let your mind wander. Commit to using metaphor and analogy during every step of the process. For instance, I use one recipe for a Berry Trifle that involves a few minutes of just staring at the freshly washed mélange of colorful berries. Don't cheat yourself by diluting the experience.

Forgive failures. Every recipe you try, just like every strategy you employ, is not always going to work. Don't look at any finished product as a failure. The activity is enough. As I mentioned earlier, "therapy begins with the first phone call," meaning that as soon as you start to think consciously about a problem, you've already started to address it. Many of us have experienced a nagging low level sense that something is wrong or dissatisfying. That's a starting point but no way to actually attack a problem. In cooking terms that's like saying "I need a dessert for the dinner party." It's not specific and you can't shop for it, let alone create it. A better plan would be, "I would like to make a tart for the dinner party." And then you may even say "an apple tart" or a "tarte Tatin." Your marital issues may mirror this example, meaning, you know something's not right and you're not happy, but you haven't really focused on what it is that's making it that way. When we use Cooking Therapy, we ask specific questions to help you crystallize the issues so you can address them. Even if the recipe you attempted does not turn out like the perfect picture in the magazine, or even as you expected, you've not wasted your time and have definitely not failed because you've been thoughtful, honest, introspective, and present.

This is about cooking as process, not food as result. There is no such thing as a failure. Pie becomes pudding, bread becomes crackers, meatloaf morphs into sloppy joes. Of course, if the dish comes out super badly, by all means, throw it out. You don't want your food, and yes, your relationship, to make you sick.

Thank you for the opportunity to come into your home and your kitchen. I wish you happy cooking, happy marriage, and happy you.

DB, The Sous Therapist.

Cook Your Financially Frustrated Marriage Happy

What is the first thing that comes to mind when you hear the term "financially frustrated marriage?" Most likely it's that one partner has unrealized expectations and disappointment. Perhaps it means that expenses are too high and income too low and either day-to-day survival is a struggle or the strain of not having enough "purchase liberty" is too great. And this is most certainly a common complaint.

But often it's not necessarily the amounts of money that stress a marriage, but the methods by which that money is managed, budgeted, or spent. You know how it goes; one is a saver and the other a spender. There may be extremely different ideas of what is "essential" and what is a luxury. Often, one partner embraces planning while another may think *budget* is a four-letter word. These are financial styles and when those styles are discordant, watch out. Financial fireworks can erupt. There is almost *nothing* that incurs more rancor and outright malice in a marriage than a financially frustrated dispute. Not kids, not in-laws, not religion. Money, sadly, trumps the others.

For the purposes of Cooking Therapy, we'll work through two of these differences. The first, as mentioned, will be disappointment. There are many reasons this may have occurred. Perhaps a career hasn't panned out or there has been a financial loss and the dreams or plans for many things, such as a home, family, or even luxury items are to be placed on hold. Perhaps one partner has built up unrealistic expectations or even been untruthful. And more and more in the current economy, job cuts, layoffs, and downsizing can occur even in the best-intended situations and with the hardest of workers. The point is often not *how* the disappointment occurs, but what part each partner thinks the other had in the disappointment. If you are secretly wondering about your partner's ability, honesty, or work ethic, chances are you are more likely to blame and resent. If your partner senses this or feels misunderstood or blamed, he or she is more likely to become defensive. When this happens, resentments build along with frustration, and if one partner believes it's bad planning or decision-making by the other, rather than bad luck, these feelings are fueled. Couple that with the "faulted" partner feeling guilt or resenting feeling guilt, and you have an explosive situation.

Unlike many other "hot topics," financial frustration can seep its way into all aspects of the marriage as it often has to do with nitty gritty survival issues like the mortgage, the monthly bills, health care, food, transportation, and tuition.

Therapists call this "coming out the neck." In other words, frustration always leaks out; if it isn't dealt with in an open and honest way, it will come out somewhere, meaning "the neck" or another argument like one about the kids or the in-laws or even the toilet seat cover. Think about a baked potato that you don't prick with the tongs of a fork. It explodes right? That's the course your marriage can take when it comes to financial frustration. We're going to start our session right away and make two recipes to deal with this first problem of disappointment and resentment. The first, is Boiling Point Volcanic Cake. No explanation necessary.

Financial frustration can seep its way into all aspects of a marriage!

Unrealized Expectations and Disappointment

BOILING POINT VOLCANIC CAKE

This recipe is modified from Paula Deen, a purposeful choice for me. Once again, a reminder that the difference between Cooking and Cooking Therapy is being purposeful, tangible, and metaphoric. This is neither support or indictment of Deen's piece in recent news, but a testament to her journey which required resilience, survival and spirit; apropos as I can get for what it takes to tackle the financially frustrated marriage.

INGREDIENTS
- 6 (1-ounce) squares bittersweet chocolate
- 2 (1-ounce) squares semisweet chocolate
- 10 tablespoons (1 ¼ stick) butter
- ½ cup all-purpose flour
- 1 ½ cups confectioners' sugar
- 3 large eggs
- 3 egg yolks
- 1 teaspoon vanilla extract
- 2 tablespoons orange or raspberry liqueur

1. Preheat oven to 425 degrees. Let's face it, for a volcanic recipe we will absolutely be using a hot oven! Take note, no doubt your arguments over money are at least 425 degrees if not hotter!

2. Grease 6 (6-ounce) custard cups. You can use ramekins or even coffee cups. What I like about this recipe is the 6 cups. Instead of one big oozing lava cake the six smaller cups represent the best beginning therapeutic practice of breaking down the problem into manageable parts. Professionals do this with every client who comes in reporting a free-flowing discontent and somewhat nebulous complaints. Until you have an idea of what the one or two (or six!) actual problems are, you can't begin to address them.

3. Melt the chocolates and butter in the microwave, or in a double boiler. What could the chocolate and butter melting together mean to you?

Think about the word melt. What have you been holding onto like a solid rock? Resentment? Blame? Could the butter and chocolate melting together take that hard rock down to something a bit less painful?

4. Add the flour and sugar to chocolate mixture. So now that you've melted a rock-hard nugget that's kept the smoothness from forming or maintaining in your marriage, it's time to add. Understanding? Forgiveness? Compassion? Think about it and you decide.

5. Stir in the eggs and yolks until smooth. I've always felt that eggs are a symbol of life, as you may agree. As you crack the whole eggs, remind yourself of a new beginning and a new life to your relationship. I often go one step further and hold each half of the egg shell palms up, hands to the sky as if giving to the life force of the universe. You may prefer a phrase, Namaste style. Perhaps you'll repeat, "Renew, Refresh, Rejoice." It's really up to you to create. As you separate the other eggs for the yolks, think about finally separating your feelings into clear and distinguishable emotions. Yes, you may be angry or sad, but don't let feelings get confused with actions of shaming, blaming, or accusing.

6. Stir in the vanilla and orange liqueur. You know the extracts and liqueurs are the spice and spirit and "something-something" of a dish. Good time to remind yourself that there may be better days ahead. Remember, you've decided to take some action and not just exist in a kind of limbo where change doesn't occur. Have a spark of hope here!

7. Divide the batter evenly among the custard cups. Place in the oven and bake for 14 minutes. The edges should be firm but the center will be runny. Don't you just love that? The edges (kind of like your new construct) will be firm, but the insides will be runny. This is the 'exploding' part of the volcanic lava cakes but instead of being out of control, you've managed to create a nice warm center.

8. Run a knife around the edges to loosen and invert onto dessert plates. I suggest a butter knife! No need for any sharper edges, you've dulled them well and it's time to 'unmold' your new concept of a relationship.

Yield: 8-10 servings.

Crumbs to Gather

We've talked quite a lot about creating in this recipe. Ultimately, the power of Cooking Therapy is concurrent with the power in you. We are all self-determining beings. You will, of course, flesh out what's transpired that got you to the point you're at, logistically (financially) and emotionally. There may well have been mistakes made, some worse than others. If laziness or absentmindedness or frivolity is involved, you will face one set of circumstances. If dishonesty has played a part, then the challenges may be greater and a deeper discussion and more intense plan may be warranted and only you can decide about the level of trust that exists or doesn't.

The power of the session is in crystallizing your own feelings and 'seeing them out there' in a way that sometimes talking about them doesn't show, and then making a comprehensive plan with additional professionals that may include, therapists, financial planners, spiritual advisors or all of the above. Now on to the next session!

Now that we've addressed the explosive nature of financial frustration, and you have some awareness of the power it can hold over your relationship's health, I want to add to the experience of letting go and enhance the first Cooking Therapy session with a second exercise.

Which is why we'll be making: You Are Not a Raspberry Fool.

I've chosen Raspberry "Fool" because feelings of shame and guilt are always present when money expectations are not met, and if not excavated and discarded, can become fossilized and embedded in resentment and arguments that can haunt a marriage for years. Whether your disappointment is fresh or cemented, it's time for an archaeological dig to remove those feelings. They are doing nothing for you. Without some acceptance of your current situation and a real willingness to let go of resentment, there is not a therapy in the world, tangible or traditional, that can help you move on.

Shame and resentment can become fossilized and haunt a marriage for years!

So, I've purposely prescribed an easy dessert, not to suggest that the task is easy, but rather, that it's clear and doable. You must commit to letting go and moving on. You must commit to letting go of the feelings that one or both of you are "a fool." Raspberry Fool is one of the simplest desserts you can make—truly a young child could handle it almost completely on their own. I know you can, too. And the metaphor is not just about a healthy and guilt-free new beginning, but also simplicity. We'll explore three aspects of simplicity as we go.

The simple fact is you are where you are.

There is some comfort in less – you can only go up!

You can begin to craft a new plan.

YOU ARE NOT A RASPBERRY FOOL

This recipe has been modified from Ree Drummond, self-described "Pioneer Woman," of the *Food Network*. Worthy of mentioning is that Ree found herself an "accidental pioneer," suddenly living out in the middle of nowhere on a ranch, not the life she planned. Rather than become mired in disappointment she transformed the unexpected into the exulted, a lesson we can all take away.

INGREDIENTS
- 3 cups raspberries, plus a few more
- ¼ cup sugar
- ½ cup confectioners' sugar
- 8 whole vanilla wafers (or other cookie)
- Fresh mint sprigs, for garnish (optional)
- 3 tablespoons raspberry liqueur (or you may just use water)
- 2 cups cold heavy cream

1. In a bowl, stir together the raspberries, sugar, and liqueur (or water) and let it sit for 10 to 15 minutes. Let's talk about this while the raspberries are 'soaking up' the sugar. I want you to think about your disappointment, your resentment and any other negative emotions related to the financial situation. They are the raspberries. You are consciously and purposefully sweetening those emotions. Look, this is the purposeful part. Can you actively let go? Can you put the raspberries 'in the past'? Each minute could represent a considerable and active move on your part to part with the past.

2. Whip the cream with the powdered sugar until soft peaks form. Transforming liquid heavy cream into whipped cream is one of the powerful metaphors in Cooking Therapy. This is an opportunity for you to start fresh and to whip lightness and sweetness into your heart—replacing a kind of liquidy and heavy substance with something light and frothy. I ask you, what would you rather your heart hold?

3. Macerate the raspberries with a fork until all the liquid and fruit are mashed together. Although you can leave some pieces of raspberry, you do want to get a nice chunky pudding like consistency. Think about no longer holding onto those large chips or boulders you've carried around for far too long! Let 'em go.

4. Spoon half the fruit into the cream and fold once or twice with a rubber spatula; do not overmix! Let's not forget color. Your visual here is white and pink; so much friendlier than the grey of disappointment.

5. Add half of the remaining fruit and fold once or twice. If you want more fruit, add the rest; if not, use remaining fruit puree as a garnish on top.

6. To serve, I suggest individual martini or other pretty glass dishes. The clarity of the glass is the metaphor, and the beauty is your reward of a new outlook. I want you to "present" yourself and/or others with this dish, with purpose and pride. You've done great work. Please top it with some crumbled cookies to represent what you've let go, and a sprig of mint, which is cool and fresh and even a little "wink" to money green.

Yield: 8 servings.

Different Financial Styles

The second concern we'll address is a difference in budgeting and spending habits. Sometimes the frustration from these style differences are bitterly entrenched, often learned in childhood either as a family norm or sometimes as a culture so abhorrent that the individual vows to do the opposite of the family norm. You've heard the phrase "when I grow up I'll never do things as my mother did," for example. Financial styles are wrought with hidden mandates about responsibility and respect and for this reason can be the most volatile triggers for a couple. It's easier to detail the different styles in story form, as we look at three "hypothetical" examples:

"You Only Go Around Once."

Carol and Howard before:

Howard had always hated the way his parents scrimped and saved and never spent on anything. Even when things broke in the house, they didn't fix them, and he grew up feeling as if he existed in a culture of wear and disrepair. He vowed that when he grew up he would always have new and expensive things and his daily mantra was "you only go around once."

Carol grew up in what she describes as a typical and average home with a dad who worked as an accountant and a stay-at-home mom. She thinks she has a healthy balance when it comes to money and while she likes her home to be clean, neat, and well-appointed, does not need to spend "unnecessarily" on luxury items.

After:

While they were dating and finances were separate, there were few problems. In fact, Carol liked the way Howard wanted to shower her with nice things and experiences. After they were married, things changed. Carol had a sense that planning for a house, family, and future required more fiscal responsibility, while Howard had absolutely no intention of changing his spending habits. As he said, he did not want to wake up and find his life had gone by and he hadn't "done anything." Howard continued to spend, acquiring top-of-the-line clothes, cars, jewelry, and home accessories while Carol was consistently thrown into the role of "angry banker." At times they would argue, but at other times Carol grew tired of the fight and would simply acquiesce. Over the years, their bank account grew very little, but

Carol's resentment skyrocketed. Their relationship suffered additionally as Howard felt resentful that Carol didn't understand his needs.

"The Future Will Take Care of Itself."

Jennifer and Jean-Paul before:

Jennifer grew up as an only child in a strict and controlling religious family. Her response to the rigidity was to become a self-proclaimed "free spirit" who wasn't weighed down by rules and convention. She escaped her rural hometown at the age of seventeen and never looked back, working temporary jobs and living modestly. Jean-Paul was attracted to Jennifer's lack of convention and artistic qualities. Having been raised in an equally structured and religious family, he admired her ability to shake free of her upbringing, readily admitting that it was not as easy for him. He said that he hoped that Jennifer "would rub off on him" but secretly he wondered how they actually would live a gypsy existence, especially as they got older, without a steady income or plan.

After:

Lingering doubts were overshadowed by the fact that Jean-Paul enjoyed everything about Jen, from her bohemian wardrobe to her lack of conformity. That was a perfect fit in their early twenties. By the time they turned 30, he began to grow weary of living hand to mouth and in short-term rental apartments, and was regretful and resentful that they'd made no plans for the future. Though he didn't exactly blame Jen, he began to recriminate about not following a more traditional career path and wondered why she didn't mirror his need to "grow up." Following Jen on her spontaneous journeys which included working on an organic co-operative farm, or as baristas at a local coffee shop and tending bar during the evenings was getting old. Every time he tried to talk to her about their lack of stability, she froze or became defensive, as these discussions triggered all of the rules and disapproval from her childhood. She reminded him that she'd never forced him to live her lifestyle and refused to feel responsible, though she actually did feel a little badly too. Still, she'd told him from day one that her philosophy was that "the future would take care of itself." Even if she wasn't as sure of that now, she certainly wasn't going to feel guilty about it.

Consequently, they moved farther and farther apart emotionally and Jean-Paul felt lost and unloved. If he couldn't get Jen to commit to some sort of blueprint for the future, Jean-Paul was seriously considering a divorce.

81

"I Want What I Want When I Want it!"

Kim and Jared before:

Kim was a stunning young woman who had been raised in an affluent family where her every desire had been indulged. She rarely heard the word "no" and because her parents traveled extensively, much of what she received for comfort, love, and nurture took the form of material possessions. On the rare occasion that she didn't get exactly what she wanted, she resorted to tantrums, sulking, isolation, and ultimately hostile or unpleasant behaviors until the situation reversed, which it often did. If Kim could not get what she wanted through her looks or influence, there was usually a member of the staff or her family who made it happen. Despite the obvious, Kim was quite bright and knew how to mask being spoiled and was a master at manipulating others to do exactly what she wanted, often making it seem as if it was their idea.

Despite his Ivy League education and financial savvy, Jared was no match for Kim's skill set. Handsome and on a fast track to hedge fund wealth, he fell hard for her charms, lifestyle, and if he was being perfectly honest, her family's substantial wealth and background. He'd grown up modestly and responsibly, but couldn't deny that it would be nice to be able to afford the finer things in life like exotic vacations and club memberships, and he ignored any nagging worries as well as overt disapproval from his family.

After:

Unfortunately, Kim's family was involved in a Ponzi scheme and within a few years of the marriage, they had lost everything. It was only Jared's career that now had the possibility of affording a luxury lifestyle, but not if Kim continued to spend as if she was, as Jared put it, "the princess of Genovia." Kim had no idea how to curb her lifestyle nor did she want to—her motto had always been, "I want what I want when I want it so I'm going to get it!" She was slowly putting the couple into deep credit card debt and Jared was stressed and sleepless.

Once in a while there are couples where one partner actually is more adult and evolved. Just as individuals have different personalities, so too, there is a continuum of emotional health. When one partner is incredibly immature, spoiled, or occluded to the idea of change despite circumstances, more serious consequences may have to occur. In this case, if Kim continues to deny and derail, Jared feels that may be the case for them.

And so, you may well be asking, what to cook?

For all three scenarios, we'll be focusing on a citrus recipe. You know how you feel when you suck on a lemon, right? Well, we're going to cook through those feelings of puckering distaste with *I'm Curdling Lemon Tart*. The original name is Lemon Curd, but because I know how couples feel when they build up outrage about spending or *not* spending, I'm certain one or both of you is *curdling*. When something curdles it has gone over the line. Most times in cooking, this ruins the dish, but there are a few exceptions, like when making candy and we bring the liquid to the hard crack stage (use your imagination here; for candy, a good thing is when its so hard it can crack into pieces. For a partnership, not so much.) Well the same is true with our lemon curd dish. We want to go over the line, just like our couples are, to the point where we've reached our limit and can't take another boiling moment! Ready?

Let's cook!

I'M CURDLING LEMON TART

This recipe is modified from Ina Garten, the Barefoot Contessa. I've been an Ina fan since she opened a store on Long Island, New York's east end in the late 1970's. Since then, she's gone on to fame and fortune and while I adore her style and talent for all things garden and food, I am awed by her love story of many years with her husband Jeffrey. Not only that, if you've ever seen Ina cook on television, you will understand the quiet Zen that Cooking Therapy can create by her on-screen presence. Her tag line, "How easy is that" belies her skill and could make world peace seem easy and the rest of us mortals believe we can accomplish similarly ambitious tasks. I've had the honor of meeting her twice, and find her as classy, friendly, and calming as any concrete therapy I've tried.

You will need a tart pan for this recipe.

If you're not a baker, it will seem a bit complicated. That's on purpose. I won't lie to you; it's going to be complicated to unravel and redo financial styles. It doesn't happen overnight and it takes methodical steps, which is exactly why I want you to take your time when you attempt this recipe. There's no sense doing it without the right tools or equipment or ingredients. And I mean that for cooking and Cooking Therapy.

INGREDIENTS

For the tart shell:
- 12 tablespoons (1 ½ sticks) unsalted butter, plus more for greasing, at room temperature
- ½ cup sugar
- 1 ¾ cups all-purpose flour
- Pinch salt
- ½ teaspoon pure vanilla extract

For the lemon curd:
- 4 lemons, at room temperature
- 1 ½ cups sugar
- ¼ pound (1 stick) unsalted butter, at room temperature
- ⅛ teaspoon salt
- 4 extra-large eggs, at room temperature

For the tart shell:

1. Mix the butter and sugar together in the bowl of an electric mixer fitted with a paddle attachment until they are just combined. Okay guys, you know how this starts. Butter and sugar and a paddle. Focus! We are taking two different substances (styles) and paddling them together! As a side note, if you do this by hand it's an excellent time to get out some frustration!

2. Add the vanilla.

3. In a medium bowl, sift together the flour and salt. So, let's talk about sifting, what a great word. This is a perfect time to "sift through" the issues. If you're the one who "only goes around once" can you only go around "once in a while" to get along? If you're the "free spirit", can you ground yourself here and there? If you've always had everything

you wanted, can you take a stab at going without? Sift through what you've always done, and what you're *willing* to do to save your relationship. Could be you end up with a smooth powder and much less of a rough patch than you imagine!

4.   Add the flour and salt mixture to the butter-and-sugar mixture. Mix on low speed until the dough starts to come together. Okay, you should be an expert at metaphor by now. Adding components, mixing nice and slow until OMG, the dough actually comes together? You got this.

5.   Dump onto a surface dusted with flour and shape into a flat disk. Press the dough into a 10-inch-round or 9-inch-square false-bottom tart pan, making sure that the finished edge is flat. Chill until firm. I swear the cooking term Ina uses is "dump." Don't you love it? I know this seems a little tricky but just think of it like this: You dumped all your "stuff" into something you can look at and shape. You're reshaping your "stuff." Just put it in the tart pan and chill. Yes, chill. Believe it or not, just like the dough, your issues don't have to be firing all the time; try chilling on them!

6.   Meanwhile, preheat the oven to 350 degrees. See, right about now we're heating things up. Which will be just what will happen when you try to make changes in your lifestyle and financial style. That's okay, heat means change and change is good.

7.   Butter one side of a square of aluminum foil to fit inside the chilled tart and place it, buttered side down, on the pastry. Fill with beans or rice to hold down. Bake for 20 minutes. Buttering up is a term you'll know. Think about that right now. When you ask your partner to change a negative pattern, please make time to compliment them for a trait you like. Butter them up for a less sticky process.

8.   Remove the foil and beans, prick the tart all over with the tines of a fork, (think of the baked potato metaphor we used earlier; sometimes things need a little "airing" so as not to crack.) Then bake again for 20 to 25 minutes more, or until lightly browned. Allow to cool to room temperature. In other words, you may have to go over and over the changes you want. Styles take a lifetime to cement, of course they're going to require repeated efforts to undo. Don't forget the cool down; without it, your "tart" will simply fall apart in your hands.

For the lemon "curdle"

1. Zest the lemons and squeeze them to make ½ cup of juice and set the juice aside. We're at the puckering part, the sour part, the bitter part. You will have to acknowledge and now's a good time, your anger and disappointment. If you're in debt, that's painful, like lemon in a paper cut! If you have to change, conform, or be more 'mainstream', that will feel sour too. But remember your choices: stay where you are with your lemons and possibly be alone, or turn them into a curdle you both can share. Up to you.

2. Put the zest in a food processor fitted with a steel blade. Add the sugar and process for 2 to 3 minutes, until the zest is very finely minced. What's this? Some sugar to the lemons? Is it possible that a little change won't kill you but may even be, (gasp), sweet?

3. In the bowl of an electric mixer fitted with a paddle attachment, cream the butter with the sugar and lemon zest. Yes, emphasis on blending, combining, meshing those very different styles into slightly more similar and "palatable" ones.

4. Add the eggs, one at a time, and then add the lemon juice and salt. Mix until combined. Once again, I always think of growth and newness when adding eggs. You should too. Your relationship is being reborn. Notice it and appreciate it and take a moment to honor it.

5. Pour the mixture into a 2-quart saucepan and cook over low heat, stirring constantly, until thickened, about 10 minutes. This is almost the last step. You've combined, paddled, added, soured, heated and heated again and now you are thickening. Change doesn't happen overnight and neither does a Lemon Curd. Well, actually, a Lemon Curd could happen overnight, but let's not lose the gist; Patience please. While it's thickening and you're stirring, stay in the moment and watch it happen. Life is a little like that; you don't see results right away but eventually, with attention, you do.

6. Finally, remove from the heat. Fill the tart shell with warm lemon curd and allow to set at room temperature. And just like that, you have a visual. As a reminder, some very different components, ones that usually don't go together, both sour and sweet, come together in a most pleasing way with work and TLC. Congratulations. Your *I'm Curdling Lemon Tart* is no longer curdling, but simply, a Lemon Curd Tart; a workable dish, just like your marriage, just like you.

Yield: Approximately 12 servings.

Clean Up (Process!)

By now you're likely to be familiar with process. Often in therapy, a therapist begins by helping the client prioritize issues, then contracting to set goals to address the most important ones. We're ahead of the game because we've already singled out one pressing issue. However, chances are that there are others; what we call co-occurring issues, and these may come up for you while participating in Cooking Therapy, because anytime you focus on a problem you're uncovering new feelings, perhaps old hurts, certainly new perspectives; think of it as an excavation.

Today we looked at your financially frustrated marriage from two perspectives. The first; disappointment and unmet expectations, and the second; different financial styles. Only you can tell if you are ready to do the work to improve any of the areas where you think you may fall. But, you should at least feel clearer, more purposeful, and more hopeful that you do have the power to address and improve your situation. I am so proud to be your Sous Therapist and of you for taking the time to try something new. You're worth it and your marriage is worth it.

Are you ready to try Cooking Therapy on your own? Keep reading.

COOKING THERAPY TAKEAWAY NOTES:

- Choose a recipe purposefully.
- Gather the ingredients your marriage needs.
- Prepare to follow new directions.
- Be thoughtful about the steps.
- Perform them mindfully,
- Expect slow change.
- Sit back, applaud your effort, and smile. You're quite the dish!

Cook Your Financially Frustrated Marriage Happy on Your Own

By using the steps above and applying them to any recipe, you can practice Cooking Therapy on your own. You can incorporate it into any regular dinner or meal. However, in order for Cooking Therapy to truly be therapeutic, you should respect it as a legitimate therapeutic modality and engage in it as you would a session with your therapist.

First, no interruptions. That means no cooking with the family running in or out, no answering the phone, no texting, and no television. The power of the therapy is focus and concentration.

Second, make an appointment with yourself for the session. Preparation is important. You wouldn't go to a therapist's office without some research and planning, so don't engage in Cooking Therapy haphazardly.

Commit. It's not okay to let your mind wander. Commit to using metaphor and analogy during every step of the process. For instance, I use one recipe for a Berry Trifle that involves a few minutes of just staring at the freshly washed mélange of colorful berries. Don't cheat yourself by diluting the experience.

Forgive failures. Every recipe you try, just like every strategy you employ, is not always going to work. Don't look at any finished product as a failure. The activity is enough. This is about cooking as process, not food as result. There is no such thing as a failure. Pie becomes pudding, bread becomes crackers, meatloaf morphs into sloppy joes. Of course, if the dish comes out super badly, by all means throw it out. You don't want your food, and yes, your relationship, to make you sick.

Thank you for the opportunity to come into your home and your kitchen. I wish you happy cooking, happy marriage, and happy you.

DB, *The Sous Therapist*.

Appendix A
(Session Recipes)

Note: Attribution for the following recipes can be found in the main text of this book, where the recipes are described in the context of therapy sessions.

A DOABLE LIFE GINGER CHICKEN RICE

INGREDIENTS
- 8 ounces chicken thigh (boneless and skinless), cut into small cubes
- 2 rice-cups short grain rice, rinsed and drained (1 rice cup is ¾ cup.)
- 1 ounce peeled ginger, sliced into needle thin (1" long)
- 1 scallion, thinly-sliced crosswise
- Toasted white sesame seeds, to taste
- 1 teaspoon sesame oil
- 1 ¼ cups dashi stock (can be substituted with chicken stock or vegetable stock)
- 2 tablespoons sake
- 1 ½ tablespoons usukuchi shoyu (light-color soy sauce) or regular soy sauce
- ½ tablespoons nampla (fish sauce; can be substituted with soy sauce).

1. In a bowl, combine the chicken, sake, soy sauce, and fish sauce, mix well by hand. Cover tightly with a plastic and let the chicken marinade for 30 minutes. It's important to stop and think about "combining." You've mingled many things in the first few months or years of your relationship; hard goods and soft. As you add each ingredient think about all the things you've blended together. And most important, USE YOUR HANDS. Your "hands" have been in this, you didn't just walk, in a daze, into your life. Take ownership of the purposeful acts you've performed.

2. Meanwhile, in the rice cooker or in the Kamado-san*, combine the rice, dashi stock, and sesame oil. Let the rice soak for 20 - 30 minutes.

I like to think about soaking when it comes to a new relationship. Sometimes your recipe has to rest or settle or congeal to come out right. Don't be so manic about fixing that you don't give the relationship time to settle into itself.

3. Spread the ginger over the rice. Add the chicken with the marinade liquid and spread on the top. This should make you think of all the good you're creating. We haven't even touched on the benefits of being with someone, sharing your life, and giving and receiving emotional support. Enjoy not being alone and coming together.

4. Cover cooker and cook over medium-high heat for 13 - 15 minutes, or until 2 - 3 minutes after the steam starts puffing out of the top lid. If you want the nice crust ("okoge") on the bottom, cook for extra 1 - 2 minutes.

5. Turn off the heat and let rest for 20 - 30 minutes. Once again, Rome wasn't built in a day. If someone works too much or is too "connected" to technology as so many are today, think about scripting real "resting" moments into the day. Cell-free dinners and Tuesday night don't be late date nights are as tangible as stirring, spicing, and covering the pot.

6. Uncover and fluff the rice. Garnish with some scallion and sesame seeds.

*This recipe calls for a Kamado-san or special rice cooker with a double lid. If you have one, great. As already discussed, however, there is no need. A heavy medium pot will do just fine. And if you customize this recipe, remember always, "One Cup Rice, Water Twice." In other words, one of you may begin this session of Cooking Therapy but it will always take "two cups" of water, to make "one cup" of your rice, turn out well.

Yield: 4-5 servings.

BLOW YOU AWAY (TWICE) BROWNIES

INGREDIENTS
- 1 cup butter (2 sticks) softened, not melted
- 2 cups sugar
- 1 ½ cups flour, self-rising for recipe #1
- 1 cup walnuts (optional)
- 4 eggs
- 4 squares unsweetened chocolate, melted (4 ounces)
- 1 teaspoon vanilla

1. Preheat oven to 350 degrees. This means you are consciously getting ready to cook. Spontaneity doesn't work in heating the oven or in addressing an issue, but planning does. Grease and flour two 8x8 pans, NO baking blend spray. Remember when we didn't have spray? It wasn't easy to butter two pans and get all those nooks and crannies and it sure was messy to flour the pans. Although not exactly painful, you will find it arduous, and when sex or even cooking is too arduous, it, too, is difficult to enjoy. Cream together butter and sugar till smooth. Okay, enough said. Take the back of the spoon and cream the butter and sugar together for a *long* time. If you've been working out it might not be so bad but probably takes a good 15-20 minutes and you will want to switch hands I suspect. Not fun.

2. Ice your sore arm. Just kidding. Kind of. Melt chocolate in top of double broiler. NO CHEATING. No microwave. This takes some time and attention, and is kind of a pain, especially to clean. Add chocolate to mixture. Again, by hand. The point is, by now you're getting the idea that this rather simple recipe takes a lot of work. You may even be in a sweat. Add eggs one at a time. You will have to do this in both recipes. Yes, there are some steps that can't be skipped in any activity.

3. Sift flour and gradually add to batter. Again, you are doing the stirring. If you haven't figured it out by now, we are going to be making *a stark* comparison about what sex (I mean brownies) may feel like now, and what it doesn't have to feel like. So now just add the vanilla and nuts. Mix and mix and mix again, then spoon equal amounts of batter into each pan. Bake for 30 minutes, approximately. Let cool and cut into squares.

Yield: 32 brownies.

BROWNIE RECIPE #2

• Same ingredients, but without pain.

1. Preheat the oven to 350 degrees. Spray the two pans with baking spray.

2. Combine softened butter (nuke to soft consistency if you need to) and sugar using paddle attachment in electric bowl stand (like a KitchenAid.) Keep mixer stirring on medium for duration.

3. Melt chocolate approximately 30 seconds in microwave and add to bowl.

4. Add eggs one at a time.

5. Sift self-rising flour and gradually add to bowl.

6. Add vanilla and nuts (if using) and add to mixture.

7. Bake for 30 minutes and let cool. Enjoy a hot cup of coffee. I suspect you're neither exhausted or depleted. In fact, you may outright feel like dancing!

Yield: 32 brownies.

BOILING POINT VOLCANIC CAKE

INGREDIENTS
- 6 (1-ounce) squares bittersweet chocolate
- 2 (1-ounce) squares semisweet chocolate
- 10 tablespoons (1 ¼ stick) butter
- ½ cup all-purpose flour
- 1 ½ cups confectioners' sugar
- 3 large eggs
- 3 egg yolks
- 1 teaspoon vanilla extract
- 2 tablespoons orange or raspberry liqueur

1. Preheat oven to 425 degrees. Let's face it, for a Volcanic recipe we will absolutely be using a hot oven! Take note, no doubt your arguments over money are at least 425 degrees if not hotter!

2. Grease 6 (6-ounce) custard cups. You can use ramekins or even coffee cups. What I like about this recipe is the 6 cups. Instead of one big oozing lava cake, the six smaller cups represent the best beginning therapeutic practice of breaking down the problem into manageable parts. Professionals do this with every client who comes in reporting free-flowing discontent and somewhat nebulous complaints. Until you have an idea of what the one or two (or six!) actual problems are, you can't begin to address them.

3. Melt the chocolates and butter in the microwave or a double boiler. What could the chocolate and butter melting together mean to you? Think about the word melt. What have you been holding onto like a solid rock? Resentment? Blame? Could the butter and chocolate melting together take that hard rock down to something a bit less painful?

4. Add the flour and sugar to chocolate mixture. So now that you've melted a rock-hard nugget that's kept the smoothness from forming or maintaining in your marriage, it's time to add. Understanding? Forgiveness? Compassion? Think about it and you decide.

5. Stir in the eggs and yolks until smooth. I've always felt that eggs are a symbol of life, as you may agree. As you crack the whole eggs,

remind yourself of a new beginning and a new life to your relationship. I often go one step further and hold each half of the egg shell palms up, hands to the sky as if giving to the life force of the universe. You may prefer a phrase, "Namaste" style. Perhaps you'll repeat, "Renew, Refresh, Rejoice." It's really up to you to create. As you separate the other eggs for the yolks, think about finally separating your feelings into clear and distinguished emotions. Yes you may be angry or sad, but don't let feelings get confused with actions of shaming, blaming, or accusing.

6. Stir in the vanilla and orange liqueur. You know the extracts and liqueurs are the spice and spirit and "something-something" of a dish. This is a good time to remind yourself that there may be better days ahead. Remember, you've decided to take some action and not just exist in a kind of limbo where change doesn't occur. Have a spark of hope here!

7. Divide the batter evenly among the custard cups. Place in the oven and bake for 14 minutes. The edges should be firm but the center will be runny. Don't you just love that? The edges (kind of like your new construct) will be firm, but the insides will be runny. This is the "exploding" part of the volcanic lava cakes, but instead of being out of control, you've managed to create a nice warm center.

8. Run a knife around the edges to loosen and invert onto dessert plates. I suggest a butter knife! No need for any sharper edges, you've dulled them well and it's time to "unmold" your new concept of a relationship.

Yield: 8-10 servings.

BREAK-UP THE BOREDOM BREAD PUDDING

INGREDIENTS
- ⅓ cup sugar
- Pinch salt
- ½ leftover loaf sweet egg bread like challah or brioche, cut into 2-inch cubes (about 5 to 6 cups)
- 2 eggs, beaten
- 2 cups milk
- 2 tablespoons (¼ stick) unsalted butter, more for greasing pan
- 1 teaspoon vanilla extract

1. Please make sure you've read the ingredients before we begin. Have you noticed all the "2"s? 2 cups milk, 2 tablespoons butter, 2 eggs... this is important. Cooking Therapy is about noticing everything! And a stale marriage is often one that's no longer noticed. This is a good time to ask: do I notice my partner? Remember, Cooking Therapy is mindful and purposeful. That's the difference between a therapy and an activity. I want you to be mindful and conscious of every step and how it resonates in life.

2. Heat oven to 350 degrees. Your marriage is not a refrigerator or no-bake cake! It needs you to turn it on. In a small saucepan over low heat warm milk, butter, vanilla, sugar, and salt. Notice you can't just turn up the flame immediately. It's a slow process that requires some attention. Continue cooking just until butter melts, allow to cool. Again, this requires some thought. You don't want to over or underdo. And when you start changing your marital patterns you may have to step back after a few changes and let things cool down.

3. Meanwhile, butter a 4-to-6-cup baking dish and fill it with cubed bread. When you were slicing and dicing the bread, what did you think about? In Cooking Therapy, everything has meaning. Perhaps the cubes represent some parts of your marriage that are currently in pieces, but at the same time you can be hopeful that the pieces will come together again. Even buttering the dish should remind you that while we want the finished product to "come together" we don't need to stick to the old ways.

4. Add eggs to cooled milk mixture and whisk. Now this is fun! Finally, you can use some energy to improve your marriage. Whisk away the old and stale till they are merely memories!) Pour mixture over bread. (As you pour, think about how much you care that your marriage improves. Pouring itself is a healing act. Notice how your efforts are soaking into everything and binding the components. Let soak for an hour. (In the recipe this is an optional step, but I include it because I think everything improves in a relationship when changes are made slowly and people have time to "soak in" those changes.

5. Bake for 30 to 45 minutes, or until custard is set but still a little wobbly and edges of bread have browned. I love this direction. A marriage isn't changed in a day. Like bread pudding, some parts have to set, some will still be wobbly and sometimes the edges remain a bit hard. Serve warm or at room temperature. At the risk of being redundant, what could be better than taking a dish from cold to warm? By now you should be smiling.

Yield: Approximately 6 servings.

I'M CURDLING LEMON TART

You will need a tart pan for this recipe.

INGREDIENTS

For the tart shell:
- 12 tablespoons (1 ½ sticks) unsalted butter, plus more for greasing, at room temperature
- ½ cup sugar1 ¾ cups all-purpose flour
- Pinch of salt
- ½ teaspoon pure vanilla extract

For the lemon curd:
- 4 lemons, at room temperature
- 1 ½ cups sugar
- ¼ pound (1 stick) unsalted butter, at room temperature
- ⅛ teaspoon salt
- 4 extra-large eggs, at room temperature

For the tart shell:

1. Mix the butter and sugar together in the bowl of an electric mixer fitted with a paddle attachment until they are just combined. Okay guys, you know how this starts. Butter and sugar and a paddle. Focus! We are taking two different substances (styles) and paddling them together!

2. Add the vanilla.

3. In a medium bowl, sift together the flour and salt. So, let's talk about sifting, what a great word. This is a perfect time to "sift through" the issues. If you're the one who "only goes around once" can you only go around "once in a while" to get along? If you're the "free spirit", can you ground yourself here and there? If you've always had everything you wanted, can you take a stab at going without? Sift through what you've always done, and what you're willing to do to save your relationship. Could be you end up with a smooth powder and much less of a rough patch than you imagine!

4. Add the flour and salt to the butter-and-sugar mixture. Mix on low speed until the dough starts to come together. Okay, you should be an expert at metaphor by now. Adding components, mixing nice and slow until OMG the dough comes together? You got this.

5. Dump onto a surface dusted with flour and shape into a flat disk. Press the dough into a 10-inch-round or 9-inch-square false-bottom tart pan, making sure that the finished edge is flat.

6. Chill until firm. I swear the cooking term Ina uses is "dump." Don't you love it? I know this seems a little tricky but just think of it like this: You dumped all your "stuff" into something you can look at and shape. You're reshaping your "stuff." Just put it in the tart pan and CHILL. Yes, chill. Believe it or not, just like the dough, your issues don't have to be firing all the time; try chilling on them!

7. Meanwhile, preheat the oven to 350 degrees. See, right about now we're heating things up. Which will be just what will happen when you try to make changes in your lifestyle and financial style. That's okay, heat means change and change is good.

8. Butter one side of a square of aluminum foil to fit inside the chilled tart and place it, buttered side down, on the pastry. Fill with beans or rice. Bake for 20 minutes. Buttering up is a term you'll know. Think about that right now. When you ask your partner to change a negative pattern, please make time to compliment them for a trait you like. Butter them up for a less sticky process.

9. Remove the foil and beans, prick the tart all over with the tines of a fork, and bake again for 20 to 25 minutes more, or until lightly browned. Allow to cool to room temperature. In other words, you may have to go over and over the changes you want. Styles take a lifetime to cement, of course they're going to require repeated efforts to undo. Don't forget the cool down; without it, your 'tart' will simply fall apart in your hands.

For the lemon "curdle"

1. Zest the lemons and squeeze them to make ½ cup of juice and set the juice aside. We're at the puckering part, the sour part, the bitter part. You will have to acknowledge, and now's a good time, your anger and disappointment. If you're in debt, that's painful, like lemon in a paper cut! If you have to change, conform, or be more "mainstream," that will feel sour too. But remember your choices; stay where you are with your lemons and possibly be alone, or turn the lemons into a curdle you both can share. Up to you.

2. Put the zest in a food processor fitted with a steel blade. Add the sugar and process for 2 to 3 minutes, until the zest is very finely minced. What's this? Some sugar to the lemons? Is it possible that a little change won't kill you but may even be, gasp, sweet?

3. In the bowl of an electric mixer fitted with a paddle attachment, cream the butter with the sugar and lemon zest. Yes, the emphasis is on blending, combining, and meshing those very different styles into slightly more similar and "palatable" ones.

4. Add the eggs, one at a time, and then add the lemon juice and salt. Mix until combined. Once again, I always think of growth and newness when adding eggs. You should too. Your relationship is being reborn. Notice it and appreciate it and take a moment to honor it.

5. Pour the mixture into a 2-quart saucepan and cook over low heat, stirring constantly, until thickened, about 10 minutes. This is almost the last step. You've combined, paddled, added, soured, heated and heated again, and now you are thickening. Rome wasn't built in a day and neither was a lemon curd. While it's thickening and you're stirring, stay in the moment and watch it happen. Life is a little like that; you don't see results right away but eventually with attention, you do.

6. Finally, remove from the heat. Fill the tart shell with warm lemon curd and allow to set at room temperature.

Yield: Approximately 12 servings.

MAKE-PEACE-NOT-WAR ISRAELI CHOPPED SALAD

INGREDIENTS

- ¼ cup minced cilantro
- ¼ cup minced mint
- ¼ cup minced parsley
- 2 teaspoons ground sumac
- 1 teaspoons ground cinnamon6 scallions, thinly sliced
- 4 cloves garlic
- 4 medium ripe tomatoes, cored, seeded, and minced
- 3 medium cucumbers, seeded and minced
- 2 serrano chilies, stemmed, seeded, and minced
- 1 red bell pepper, stemmed, seeded, and minced
- Kosher salt and freshly ground black pepper, to taste
- 1 large white onion, minced
- ½ cup olive oil
- Juice and zest of 3 lemons

Mix all the ingredients in a bowl. Let sit 20 minutes before serving.
Yield: Approximately 5 servings.

Well, how'd it go? Did you feel purposeful and productive? Many people report that the worst thing about struggling in a relationship is a sense of not being able to do something. I've chosen a recipe for you that is highly structured and directive and combats that, as no doubt you now well know. There is much to do in this recipe just like your relationship.

Alternately, did it feel endless and impossible and not worth it? You will have to explore that and make the connection. This is not to say that making a salad and your feelings around it are a prescription to keep or discard a marriage; but it is information.

MASTERBAKETION: NO TRIFLING THING

INGREDIENTS

For the pudding:

- ½ cup white sugar
- 3 tablespoons unsweetened cocoa powder
- ¼ cup cornstarch
- ⅛ teaspoon salt
- 2 tablespoons butter, room temperature
- 1 teaspoon vanilla extract
- 2 ¾ cups milk
- Shot of bourbon or amaretto (optional)

For layering the trifle:

- 1 store bought pound or angel food cake cut into cubes
- 1 cup each exotic fruit (like kiwi and mango)

1. In a saucepan, stir together sugar, cocoa, cornstarch, and salt. Place over medium heat and stir in milk. Bring to a boil and cook, stirring constantly, until mixture thickens enough to coat the back of a metal spoon. The stirring is the key here. Although this is a simple recipe, the stirring is so important that it's the difference between success and the garbage pail. Purposefully focus on what you are doing. By stirring or keeping things moving, you are not allowing the mixture to get clumpy or burned. Just like in a marriage, this dish requires your total attention for a short time. That is giving to the dish and being present in the act.

2. You are also stirring up some of your own emotions! Go with it and have fun. As you run the spoon around the pot can you think about what makes you warm and fluid inside? And if you happen to feel stirrings from the stirrings? Hold that thought for later!

3. Remove from heat, and stir in the butter and vanilla. Stir in liquor if you're feeling naughty and that is naughty in a good way! Let cool briefly. Then chill in refrigerator until ready to compose.

4. When chilled, stir a little pudding in the bottom of a trifle dish or large glass bowl. Then layer cake, pudding, and fruit 2 to 3 times.

5. When the trifle is set, take a moment to think about the many layers involved. Think about the pudding and the textures it takes and how that mirrors the emotions in a relationship. You can start with something watery and diluted, with separate parts, and stir together a creation that's harmonious, thickened, both hot and cold, both soft and together, both tantalizing and satisfying. Pudding. Marriage. So close.

Yield: Approximately 10 servings.

NEITHER CUCKOO, NOR COCONUTS, CAKE

INGREDIENTS

Filling:
- 2 tablespoons cornstarch½ cup sugar
- ½ cup unsalted butter
- 2 ¼ cups sweetened flaked coconut
- ¼ cup sour cream
- 2 tablespoons water
- 1 teaspoon vanilla extract
- 1 ¼ cups whipping cream

Cake:
- 3 ½ cups all-purpose flour
- 1 tablespoon baking powder
- ½ teaspoon salt
- 2 ¼ cups sugar
- 1 ½ cups unsalted butter, room temperature
- 5 large eggs
- 1 1/3 cups whipping cream
- 1 tablespoon vanilla extract

Frosting:
- 2 (8 ounce) packages cream cheese, room temperature
- ½ cup unsalted butter, room temperature
- 2 cups powdered sugar
- 4 cups sweetened flaked coconut, toasted
- 1 teaspoon vanilla extract

Filling:
1. Stir cornstarch, 2 tablespoons water, and vanilla in small bowl to dissolve cornstarch. As you remember, we spoke about in terms of changing habits in a way your partner can hear. Just like this first step, think too, about the word "dissolve". It's a big one. You have the power to "dissolve" tension or to let your exchanges "dissolve" into anger.

2. Bring cream, sugar, and butter to boil in heavy medium saucepan. This takes a bit of patience, right? Remember number two on the Quirks list? Someone is buying gifts that the other person really doesn't want. Hmmm, instead of focusing on what the gifts are, how about the sentiment behind them? Someone is buying things for you they think will make you happy! Chances are a year ago that wasn't happening. Chances are you'd never boil up a bowl of cream, sugar, and butter, either, but at the end of the day you're going to have cake. And a person who thinks of the other person and gets them trinkets to say so? Kind of like getting cake.

3. Add cornstarch mixture and bring to boil. Remove from heat and stir in coconut. Cool completely. I can't stress these steps enough. Maybe your parents said it: never go to sleep on a fight. I promise you that if you don't react too quickly, your relationship will always go better. Just like this filling. If it went into a cake now it would run and seep out, accomplishing nothing. So, mix in the sour cream (a little patience and thought) and chill. Mix in sour cream. Cover and refrigerate overnight.

Cake:

Preheat oven to 325 degrees.

1. Butter and flour 3 9-inch round cake pans. Let's talk about the number 3. This is quite the layer cake, right? Well your marriage is made up of many layers, too. And trust me, three is not all that many! For now, it's the two of you and the newness, but later, and as you grow together you'll encounter layers that will test you. Remember this time, this simpler time, when it was ONLY three layers!

2. Whisk flour, baking powder, and salt in large bowl to blend.

3. Using electric mixer, beat sugar and butter in another large bowl to blend. These two steps give you an opportunity to think about difference and blending. One bowl has the dry ingredients, another the butter blend. Separate pieces that will fold into each other to form something better.

4. Add eggs one at a time, beating well after each addition. For each egg, go back to the list in your mind. Can you deal with loud laughter? Funny sneeze? Tofu ice cream? I bet you can.

5. Beat in cream and vanilla.

6. Stir flour mixture into butter mixture.

7. Divide batter equally among pans. Dividing the batter into equal pans should promote a sense of organization and balance. You can and should want to be each equally present in the relationship. Three pans, three representations; you, your partner, and the marriage. Because the marriage is a living breathing soul that needs to be nurtured.

8. Bake until tester inserted into center of cakes comes out clean, about 35 minutes. Cool completely. This is a good time to talk about late vs. early, technically a minor difference but one of those that can become a real problem. Just as we wouldn't take the cake out early, you will have to negotiate time preferences with your partner. In a perfect world, you'd have a talk with your mate and you'd meet in the middle and it would all work out, but we know it doesn't usually end up that way. People have their own inner clocks. So, you may have to get creative the way a baker might. For instance, bakers use the freezer or an ice bath to accelerate cooling. Perhaps you have to tell your partner the reservation is for 7 pm when it's really 7:30 pm. Or perhaps you need to set your watch ahead. This is not avoiding a solution, its self-preservation! Just ask anyone who's crossed the hump of the new marriage. Sometimes you just have to do what works.

Frosting:

1. Using electric mixer, beat cream cheese and butter in large bowl to blend. Remember how we talked about something like laughter? Hers too irritating, his too loud? Here we need that annoying loud beater to get to the delicious frosting. If you look at it that way, somewhat less annoying and more something to be embraced. Maybe you could try that with your partner, you know, the one over there you love and adore?

2. Beat in powdered sugar and vanilla extract. Place one cake layer on cake plate. Top with half of filling.

3. Place second cake layer atop filling. Top with remaining filling.

4. Place third cake layer atop filling.

5. Spread frosting over top and sides of cake. Pat toasted coconut over top and sides of cake, pressing gently to adhere.

6. Cover and refrigerate. Let stand at room temperature 3 hours before serving. Can be prepared up to 1 day ahead.

Yield: 12 servings.

NO MORE MONOTONY MEATLOAF

INGREDIENTS

Loaf:
- 1½ cups soft bread crumbs (2 slices)
- ½ cup finely chopped celery
- 2 tablespoons finely chopped onion
- 1 pond ground beef (or turkey)
- Salt and pepper, to taste
- 1 egg, beaten
- 1 teaspoon Dijon mustard

Topping:
- 1 tablespoon brown sugar
- ½ cup applesauce
- 1 ½ teaspoon vinegar (apple cider vinegar preferred)
- ½ teaspoon Dijon mustard

1. Once again, we need to preheat the oven to 350 degrees. And once again, remind yourself that making changes, and in fact, heating anything takes time and happens slowly. Notice that the recipe has two parts. One goes before and one goes after. Begin to think about how you were doing things before this day, and how you're going to do things differently, or "top it off" going forward.

2. Combine all ingredients that go into the loaf. When a recipe calls for combining several ingredients, the tendency is to short circuit your focus on each. Let's avoid that here. When beating the eggs think about them metaphorically for your communication skills, or the way you approach subjects. Do you beat them to death? Does that work? Do you under beat? Either way do they achieve the result you want? Beating takes patience, just as finely chopping the celery and the onion. Will you rush through or take your time? In this recipe, which calls for Dijon mustard and brown sugar, the amounts are important. Use the moment to ask yourself, what amounts of sweet or cynical do I put into my relationship. What about my partner? Sometimes Cooking Therapy is simply diagnostic and the basis for more work.

3. Mix thoroughly. As all chefs know, there is just no other way to make meatloaf or meatballs without using your hands. Yep, you have to get in there and do the dirty work. It's messy and cold and sometimes downright disgusting. Yes, I am talking about marriage. Also, meatloaf. But remember, at the end you get something just dense enough, just soft enough, and hopefully delicious.

4. Shape into a round loaf. There's really nothing more powerful than comparing your work at "shaping" a meatloaf to your work at shaping your part of a relationship. This loaf does not require perfection and neither do you. The recipe calls for shaping the mixture into a round loaf in a square pan. Just do your best.

5. Make a depression in the top of the loaf leaving about 1 inch around.

6. Combine topping ingredients and pour into depression. Okay I really hate to use the word "depression" in an upbeat session of Cooking Therapy but we can "mine" the metaphor to acknowledge that marital monotony can be depressing, and if left untreated, can lead to more serious or clinical issues. So, when you make that depression please concentrate on the fact that you are *filling* it with something, and in this case, something sweet. Then bake the loaf for 1 hour, which will seal in the sweetness and your efforts.

Yield: 4 servings.

TUNE-IN AND TALK TO ME TACOS!

INGREDIENTS

- Any pre-packaged taco package that offers both hard and soft taco shells
- 1 pound of ground beef and 1 pound of either chicken or turkey
- 2 packages grated cheese of your choice
- 10 toppings of your choice*

*Some ideas are tomatoes, lettuce, onions, green and black olives, salsa, sour cream, scallions, guacamole, etc. Some people shave chocolate into their tacos to simulate a Mole sauce. The toppings are up to you, but I want a full ten!

1. Take out two saucepans and put the beef in one and the poultry in the other. The idea here is to think about satisfying two people. If, however, you know for sure that you both like one or the other, making only one is fine. More on this later.

2. Sauté as per the box directions, splitting (if you have two proteins), and adding the taco seasoning. As you do, I want you to think quite consciously about the word seasoning. What does it do? It adds a particular flavor, spice and depth, no? And aren't those two ingredients necessary for any relationship?

3. Drain your protein and reserve. Look, so many culinary functions have metaphors for life, don't they? Think about reduction, concentration, caramelization, essence. But 'drain' can be super powerful! As the excess liquid goes out of the dish, remind yourself that you're willing to lose what dilutes your marriage, and reserve the best of everything.

4. Arrange the toppings in your Lazy Susan or in your bowls or mugs. Arrange them in a circle if possible to signify, like a circle, that your marriage cannot be broken.

5. As per the package directions, heat up both hard and soft tacos. You are going to make a taco out of the one you like *most*! Stay with me here. Remember we talked about not communicating your needs and building up resentment and frustration? Here is where you first make a taco exactly to your liking. This is *your* taco, exactly how you like it. You don't have the chicken because there's not enough beef.... you don't skimp on the ingredients you love for any reason. This is your taco. Go ahead, I'll wait! So delicious right? It feels good to get what you want. That's good selfishness. It makes you a content and

fulfilled person who isn't frustrated and wants others to be happy too. And by the way, content and happy people feel sexy and more intimate.

6. And now comes the compromise. You are going to make a second taco with the shell you like least. Yep, least. But don't panic, I'm not going to make you eat an entire taco filled with things you don't like. I'm going to ask you to add three things you wouldn't normally add but that your partner would. It's the honor system. And as you eat the taco, I'll bet you'll be pleasantly surprised. Compromise is almost never as bad as you think. And while this one is forced, it has what I call "legs." Let me explain:

Yield: 12-16 servings, depending on brand.

YOU ARE NOT AN ICEBOX CAKE (I)

INGREDIENTS
- 1 package (9 ounces) chocolate wafers
- 2 cups whipping cream
- 1 teaspoon vanilla

1. Beat whipping cream on high until stiff peaks form. There are so many sexual innuendos in that one instruction I think I'm going to simply leave you to it. Just remember, when you give your playful, active self to a task and to your marriage, you are more likely to get the same in return.

2. Gently stir in vanilla. Of course, your marriage requires your tender touch.

3. Spread 1 ½ teaspoon whipped cream onto each cracker. Stack. Take your time. The only labor in this recipe comes from being methodical at this moment for a short time.

4. Lay stack on side on platter and cover with whipped cream. This slightly delicate move should remind you of your creativity, commitment to the "shape" of your marriage going from something forgotten and left to something formed with care.

5. Chill 4 hours or more.

Yield: 14 servings.

YOU ARE NOT A RASPBERRY FOOL

INGREDIENTS
- 3 cups raspberries, plus a few more
- ¼ cup sugar
- ½ cup confectioners sugar
- 8 whole vanilla wafers (or other cookie)
- Fresh mint sprigs, for garnish (optional)
- 3 tablespoons raspberry liqueur (or you may just use water)
- 2 cups cold heavy cream

1. In a bowl, stir together the raspberries, sugar, and liqueur (or water) and let it sit for 10 to 15 minutes. Let's talk about this while the raspberries are "soaking up" the sugar. I want you to think about your disappointment, your resentment, and any other negative emotions related to the financial situation. They are the raspberries. You are consciously and purposefully sweetening those emotions. Look, this is the purposeful part. Can you actively let go? Can you put the raspberries "in the past?" Each minute could represent a considerable and active move on your part to part with the past.

2. Whip the cream with the powdered sugar until soft peaks form. Transforming liquid heavy cream into whipped cream is one of the powerful metaphors in Cooking Therapy. This is an opportunity for you to start fresh and to whip lightness and sweetness into your heart—replacing a kind of liquid-y and heavy substance with something light and frothy. I ask you, what would you rather your heart hold?

3. Mash the raspberries with a fork until all the liquid and fruit are mashed together. Macerate would be a better word for this. Although you can leave some pieces of raspberry, you do want to get a nice chunky pudding like consistency. Think about no longer holding onto those large chips or boulders you've carried around for far too long! Let 'em go.

4. Spoon half the fruit into the cream and fold once or twice with a rubber spatula; do not over mix! Let's not forget color. Your visual here is white and pink; so much friendlier than the grey of disappointment.

5. Add half of the remaining fruit and fold once or twice. If you want more fruit, add the rest; if not, use remaining fruit puree as a garnish on top. To serve, I suggest individual martini or other pretty glass dishes. The clarity of the glass is the metaphor, and the beauty is your reward of a new outlook. I want you to "present" yourself and/or others with this dish, with purpose and pride. You've done great work. Please top it with some crumbled cookies to represent what you've let go, and a sprig of mint, which is cool, fresh, and even a little "wink" to money green.

Yield: 8 servings.

Appendix B
(Extra Recipes)

BESAME (KISS ME) BECHAMEL SAUCE
Recipes from The Fannie Farmer Cookbook

INGREDIENTS
- 2 tablespoons butter
- 2 tablespoons flour
- Salt, to taste
- Freshly ground pepper, to taste
- 1 ¼ cups milk, heated

Melt the butter in a heavy-bottomed saucepan. Stir in the flour and cook, stirring constantly, until the paste cooks and bubbles a bit, but don't let it brown — about 2 minutes. Add the hot milk, continuing to stir as the sauce thickens. Bring it to a boil. Add salt and pepper to taste, lower the heat, and cook, stirring for 2 to 3 minutes more. Remove from the heat. To cool this sauce for later use, cover it with wax paper or pour a film of milk over it to prevent a skin from forming.

Yield: 12 servings.

BECHAMEL CHEESE SAUCE

INGREDIENTS
- Besame (Kiss Me) Bechamel Sauce
- ½ cup cheddar cheese
- Cayenne pepper, to taste

1. Stir in ½ cup grated Cheddar cheese during the last 2 minutes of cooking, along with a pinch of cayenne pepper.
2. Warm the milk on low heat just until little bubbles begin to form at the edges. Then remove from heat.

Yield: About 1 cup.

CARAMEL COUPLE IN A CRUNCH CANDIES
Recipe by Marcy Goldman

This recipe was originally passed on to me by my cousin Dena but I've come to learn that most people are familiar with it despite not knowing the origin. A version made for the Jewish holiday of Passover uses matzo and is credited to Marcy Goldman.

INGREDIENTS
- Escort Crackers, enough to cover the bottom of a 10" x 15" cookie sheet
- 1 cup (2 sticks) unsalted butter
- 1 cup firmly packed brown sugar
- ¼ cup coarsely chopped chocolate, semi-sweet chocolate, or white chocolate, chips okay to use

1. Preheat the oven to 375 degrees. Use foil baking sheet or line sheet completely with foil. Cover the foil with baking parchment. This is very important since the mixture becomes sticky during baking.

2. Line the bottom of the cookie sheet evenly with the crackers, as many as you need to fit.

3. In a 3-quart, heavy-bottomed saucepan, combine the butter and brown sugar.

4. Cook over medium heat, stirring constantly, until the mixture comes to a boil (about 2 to 4 minutes). Boil for 3 minutes, stirring constantly.

5. Remove from the heat and pour over the crackers, covering completely.

6. Place the baking sheet in the oven and immediately reduce the heat to 350 degrees. Bake for 15 minutes, checking every few minutes to make sure the mixture is not burning (if it seems to be browning too quickly, remove the pan from the oven, lower the heat to 325 degrees, and replace the pan).

7. Remove from the oven and sprinkle immediately with the chopped chocolate or chips. Let stand for 5 minutes, then spread the melted chocolate over the crackers. While still warm, break into squares or odd shapes. Chill, still in the pan, in the freezer until set.

Yield: Approximately 30 pieces.

CHILL ON IT ICEBOX CAKE (II)

Recipe by Nabisco

INGREDIENTS

- 2 tablespoons confectioners' sugar
- 1 (9 ounce) package chocolate wafer cookies
- ¼ cup grated chocolate
- 1 ½ cups heavy whipping cream
- 2 teaspoons vanilla extract

1. Beat cream in a large glass or metal mixing bowl with an electric mixer. Gradually add confectioners' sugar and vanilla extract, continuing to beat until the cream holds stiff peaks. Lift your beater or whisk straight up; the whipped cream should form a sharp peak that holds its shape.

2. Spread a generous teaspoon of whipped cream on each cookie. Press cookies together to make 3-inch stacks.

3. Spread a 1-inch wide line of whipped cream down center of a serving platter. Assemble cookie stacks into a log on platter following the line of whipped cream.

4. Frost cookie log with remaining whipped cream and sprinkle with grated chocolate.

5. Cover tightly and refrigerate overnight.

6. To serve, slice diagonally to create striped pieces.

Yield: 14 servings.

DON'T WORRY, BE HAPPY PIE

Old Family Recipe

INGREDIENTS
- 1 package of soft ladyfingers
- 2 large boxes of chocolate pudding mix (instant or not, your choice)
- 1 pint heavy whipping cream

1. Line the bottom of a 9 x 13 Pyrex dish with ladyfingers, insides facing up.
2. Prepare pudding as directed, let cool just slightly, spread over ladyfingers.
3. Whip cream, adding a touch of sugar if you prefer, and spread on top of all*.
4. Chill for several hours and enjoy.

*You may layer bananas over chocolate if you like.

Yield: 1 pie.

FROM BOILING TO BLISS CAKE

Recipe from Bon Appétit

INGREDIENTS
- 4 pints dulce de leche ice cream
- 2 pints strawberry sorbet
- 2 ½ pounds strawberries, sliced
- Purchased caramel sauce, as needed (optional)

1. Preheat the oven to 350 degrees.
2. Melt butter in medium saucepan over medium-high heat.
3. Stir in brown sugar. Bring to a boil. Boil 2 minutes.
4. Remove from heat. Stir in pecans.
5. Press mixture over bottom (not sides) of 10-inch-diameter spring form pan.
6. Bake 10 minutes. Cool 30 minutes or until cooled.
7. Bake crust until golden, about 8 minutes. Cool completely.
8. Slightly soften 1 ¼ pints ice cream; spread over crust. Freeze until firm, about 1 hour.
9. Slightly soften 1 pint sorbet and spread over ice cream. Freeze until firm, about 30 minutes.
10. Slightly soften 1 ¼ pints ice cream, spread over sorbet. Freeze until firm, about 1 hour.
11. Slightly soften 1 pint sorbet; spread over ice cream. Freeze until firm, about 30 minutes.
12. Slightly soften 1 ½ pints ice cream; spread over sorbet for top layer.
13. Cover; freeze until firm, at least 3 hours and up to 1 week.
14. Stir berries and ⅓ cup sugar in large bowl. Let stand until berries release their juices, about 30 minutes.
15. Cut around cake to loosen. Release pan sides.
16. Cut cake into wedges; arrange on plates.
17. Spoon berries atop wedges; drizzle with caramel sauce, if desired.

Yield: About 16 servings.

GRANDMA'S BAKED ZITI

Recipe by Donna Selman

INGREDIENTS
- 1 pound dry ziti
- 1.5-2 pounds ricotta cheese
- 2 cups shredded mozzarella cheese
- ¼ cup grated parmesan
- 1 32-ounce jar spaghetti sauce or homemade

1. Cook ziti according to directions. Add sauce and first two cheeses. Sprinkle with parmesan.
2. Layer into a 9x13 Pyrex baking dish.
3. Bake 25 minutes covered at 350 degrees.

Yield: 24 side servings.

JUST ROLL WITH IT DUDE CALIFORNIA ROLLS

Recipe by Palatablepastime.com

INGREDIENTS
- ½ sheet toasted nori
- ⅓ cup prepared sushi rice
- 1 ounce sashimi grade tuna, sliced
- 2 pieces peeled English cucumbers (2 to 3 matchstick-sized pieces)
- 2 pieces sliced avocados (2 to 3)
- 1 ½ teaspoons wasabi powder
- 1 tablespoon pickled ginger (optional)
- 1 tablespoon grated daikon radish (optional)
- 1 ½ teaspoons mayonnaise
- 1 teaspoon wasabi paste (optional)
- 1 tablespoon soy sauce (optional)

1. Place toasted nori (shiny side down) on rolling mat.
2. Cover center of nori with sushi rice.
3. Mix together mayo with wasabi powder to make wasabi mayo.
4. Spread wasabi mayo over rice.
5. Place a row of tuna, cucumber, and avocado over rice.
6. Roll up nori using mat, and moisten the farthest edge of exposed nori to form a seal.
7. Slice into serving pieces.
8. Serve garnished with pickled ginger, daikon radish, wasabi, and soy sauce, if desired.

Yield: About 6 servings.

LIFE IS SWEET AND SOUR MEATBALLS
Old Family Recipe

An old family recipe that I know by heart, no pun intended.

INGREDIENTS
- 1 pound any chopped meat (beef traditionally, turkey is just fine)
- ½ cup flavored breadcrumbs or panko
- 1 egg
- 1 jar of chili sauce (I use Heinz)
- 1 small jar of red currant jam (can use black currant or jelly in a pinch and I've used cranberry sauce too!)
- ½ cup cooking sherry

1. Mix meat, breadcrumbs or panko, and egg together by hand and form into size meatballs of choice. Smaller are traditionally called cocktail meatballs. If you're of age, feel free to have a cocktail while making! Combine chili sauce, jam, and cooking sherry in a large pot that will hold meatballs.

2. Bring to a boil then lower heat, add meatballs, simmer uncovered 45 minutes.

Yield: Approximately 40 cocktail size meatballs.

MISS YOU MUCHO MINI MUFFINS

Old Family Recipe

INGREDIENTS

- 1 8-ounce package cream cheese, softened (can use light)
- ⅓ cup sugar
- 1 12-ounce package chocolate chips, or to taste
- 1 ½ cups flour
- ¼ cups cocoa
- ⅛ teaspoon salt
- 1 teaspoon baking soda
- 1 egg
- 1 cup water
- ⅓ cup cooking oil
- 1 teaspoon vanilla

1. Preheat the oven to 350 degrees.

2. Mix together cream cheese and sugar, then add egg and mix well. Fold in chocolate chips and put aside.

3. Sift together flour, sugar, cocoa, baking soda, and salt. Add water and mix, slowly adding oil and vanilla. Use miniature cupcake tins with miniature fillers and fill each one* about halfway full with chocolate mixture, then top with 1 teaspoon of cheese mixture.

4. Bake for 20 minutes or until starting to become golden. Recipe can be frozen.**

Yield: approximately 4 dozen.

*Hint: If you can find a squeeze bottle and cut the opening wider, it is easier to fill that way. Or learn to use a pastry bag. Otherwise, you just have to do it using a ladle and get the feel of it. It's messy, don't worry about it.

**Options: you can crumble nuts on top, any kind you want (you can even dye them in food coloring if you want color — I did this once for Halloween) or use white chocolate.

Yield: Approximately 4 dozen muffins.

NANNY'S MATZAH BREI

Old Family Recipe

INGREDIENTS
- 6 pieces matzah
- ¼ cup butter or non-stick spray for pan
- 4 eggs
- ¼ cup milk
- 1 teaspoon vanilla

1. Place butter on large skillet or spray with non-stick spray and heat on medium-high heat.

2. Break matzah into pieces and cover with water in bowl. Soak for 10 minutes until soft.

3. Drain matzah well and squeeze out excess with dish towel.

4. In separate bowl beat eggs, add milk and vanilla, and stir well.

5. Pour egg mixture over softened matzah and let absorb for a few minutes.

6. Lay mixture in single flat layer if possible to fill pan.

7. Cook on one side for approx. 5-10 minutes or until golden brown. Carefully flip matzah (can do in sections) and brown other side, making sure eggs are cooked and not raw.

8. Remove from pan onto large plate or platter.

9. Serve with sugar, jelly, or syrup!

Yield: 6 servings.

PLAN TO MAKE IT WORK MAC AND CHEESE

Recipe from Thepudgefactor.com

INGREDIENTS
- 2 cups (8 ounces) uncooked elbow macaroni
- 1 tablespoon unsalted butter, room temperature
- 3 ounces cream cheese, room temperature
- 1 tablespoon dry mustard
- 2 cups (8 ounces) shredded Cheddar cheese, divided
- 2 cups (8 ounces) shredded Fontina cheese, divided
- Salt, to taste
- Freshly ground black pepper, to taste
- ¼ cup panko bread crumbs
- 1 cup (8 ounces) milk
- 1 large egg
- 1 tablespoon olive oil

1. Preheat oven to 350 degrees. Generously butter cups of muffin pan. Set aside.
2. Cook macaroni in salted boiling water for 7 minutes. Drain in colander. Transfer to large mixing bowl.
3. Add butter and cream cheese to hot macaroni. Stir to melt butter and cream cheese and evenly coat macaroni.
4. Add milk and egg; stir to evenly coat macaroni.
5. Add dry mustard, ¼ to ½ teaspoon of salt, and ⅛ teaspoon freshly ground black pepper; stir to combine.
6. Add 1½ cups cheddar cheese and 1½ cups Fontina cheese; stir to combine.
7. Spoon macaroni mixture into muffin pan. Top with reserved cheddar cheese and Fontina cheese.
8. Mix Panko bread crumbs with 1 tablespoon olive oil. Sprinkle 1 teaspoon of Panko bread crumb mixture on top of macaroni cups.
9. Bake in preheated oven for 30 to 35 minutes, or until tops are golden brown and bubbly, and macaroni is set.
10. Remove from oven; cool 10 minutes before removing from pan to wire rack to continue cooling.

May be served hot or cold, refrigerated and reheated, or frozen and reheated.
Yield: About 12 servings.

SALMON WITH A SIDE OF SELF ESTEEM

Recipe from Allrecipes.com

INGREDIENTS

- ¾ cup wasabi peas (about 3 ounces)
- 4 (8-ounce) salmon fillets with skin (each about 1 inch to 1 ¼ inches thick)
- 1 tablespoon finely grated lime peel
- Lime wedges
- 2 tablespoons olive oil, divided
- 2 tablespoons fresh lime juice

1. Preheat oven to 400 degrees. Blend wasabi peas in processor until ground but with some coarsely crushed pieces. Lightly oil rimmed baking sheet. Arrange salmon fillets, skin side down, on prepared baking sheet. Sprinkle fish with salt. Press ground wasabi peas onto tops of salmon fillets to adhere, covering tops completely. Sprinkle grated lime peel over salmon; drizzle with 1 tablespoon oil. Roast salmon just until opaque in center, about 10 minutes.

2. Transfer 1 salmon fillet to each of 4 plates. Drizzle with lime juice. Garnish with lime wedges and serve.

Yield: 4 servings.

SESAME NEWDLES

Recipes from The Silver Palate Cookbook

INGREDIENTS

- 1 pound thin linguine or other thin pasta
- 8 scallions, trimmed, well rinsed, and cut diagonally into ½ inch pieces
- Thinly sliced red pepper for color (optional)
- Blanched asparagus tips, broccoli florets, or snow peas, for garnish (optional)
- ¼ cup peanut oil
- 2 cups sesame mayonnaise (recipe follows)
- A few drops of Szechuan hot chili oil to taste (look for it in the Asian food section)

1. Bring 4 quarts of salted water to a boil in a large pot. Drop in the linguine and cook until tender, but still firm. Drain, toss in a mixing bowl with the peanut oil, and let cool to room temperature.

2. Whisk together the sesame mayonnaise and drops of the chili oil, to taste, in a small bowl. Do not hesitate to make it quite spicy; the noodles will absorb a lot of heat.

3. Add the scallions to the pasta, pour in the sesame mayonnaise, and toss gently. Cover and refrigerate until serving time. (Better if made day before or longer)

4. Toss the noodles again and add additional sesame mayonnaise if they seem dry. Arrange in a serving bowl and garnish with the asparagus, broccoli, or snow peas. Serve at room temperature (preferred) or cold.

Yield: 6 servings as a main dish.

SESAME MAYONNAISE

INGREDIENTS

- 1 whole egg
- 2 egg yolks
- 2 ½ tablespoons rice vinegar (in Asian food section of market)
- 2 ½ tablespoons soy sauce
- 3 tablespoons Dijon mustard
- ¼ cup dark sesame oil (in Asian food section of market)
- 2 ½ cups of corn or vegetable oil (I always cut the corn oil down to 1.5 or 2 cups and it tastes just fine)
- Szechuan style hot chili oil, to taste (optional, in Asian food section of market)

1. In a food processor or blender, process the whole egg, egg yolks, vinegar, soy sauce, and mustard for 1 minute.

2. With the motor still running, dribble in the sesame oil and then the corn oil in a slow, steady stream.

3. Season with drops of the chili oil if you use it, and scrape the mayonnaise into a bowl. Cover and refrigerate until ready to use.

Yield: 3 ½ cups.

STOP AND SMELL THE BERRIES PIE

Recipe from Allrecipes.com

INGREDIENTS

Pastry for a Double-Crust Pie:

• 2 cups all-purpose flour

• ½ teaspoon salt

• 2/3 cup shortening, chilled

• 6 tablespoons cold water

Three-Berry Filling:

• 1 cup fresh strawberries, halved

• 2 cups fresh raspberries

• 1 ½ cups fresh blueberries

• ½ cup white sugar

• 3 tablespoons cornstarch

1. Combine the flour and salt. Using a pastry blender, cut in the shortening until the pieces are the size of small peas. Sprinkle 1 tablespoon of the water over part of the mixture, then gently toss with a fork. Push moistened portion to the side of the bowl. Repeat, using 1 tablespoon of water at a time, until all is moistened. Divide the dough in half. Form each half into a ball and flatten slightly. Wrap in plastic and refrigerate for at least 30 minutes.

2. Transfer one piece of dough to a lightly floured surface. Roll the dough from the center to the edges to form a 12-inch circle. Wrap the crust around the rolling pin. Unroll it onto a 9-inch pie plate. Ease the crust into the pie plate, being careful not to stretch it. Trim the bottom crust evenly with the rim of the pie plate, and return the pastry-lined pie plate to the refrigerator.

3. In a large mixing bowl, stir together the sugar and cornstarch. Add the strawberries, raspberries, and blueberries; gently toss until berries are coated. Allow fruit mixture to stand for about 15 minutes.

4. Preheat the oven to 375 degrees. Place a baking sheet in the oven to preheat.

5. Roll out the remaining pastry for the top crust. Stir the berry mixture

and pour the filling into the pastry-lined pie plate. Place the top crust over the pie and trim the edges, leaving a ½-inch overhang. Fold the top crust under the bottom crust, pressing lightly to seal. Crimp the edges of the crust and cut vents in the top to allow steam to escape. To prevent over-browning, cover the edge of the pie with foil.

6. Bake in the preheated oven on the baking tray for 25 minutes. Remove the foil.

7. Bake for an additional 20 to 30 minutes, or until the filling is bubbling and the crust is golden. Cool on a wire rack.

Yield: 1 pie.

THERE'S THE RUB RUB

Recipe by chefworks.com

Use this rub on the backyard barbecue dish of your choice!

INGREDIENTS

- ½ cup brown sugar
- ¼ cup paprika
- 1 tablespoon black pepper
- 1 tablespoon salt
- 1 tablespoon chili powder
- 1 tablespoon garlic powder
- 1 tablespoon onion powder
- 1 teaspoon cayenne pepper
- ¼ teaspoon curry powder

You can mix and match almost all of the spices in this rub to highlight or eliminate flavors.

Yield: Approximately 1 cup.

YOUR CUP OF TEA CUPCAKES

Recipe from Real Simple

This is a basic cupcake recipe from *Real Simple*. You get to customize the additions and toppings.

INGREDIENTS
- 3 ½ cups all-purpose flour, spooned and leveled
- 1 cup (2 sticks) unsalted butter, at room temperature, plus more for the pan(s)
- 1 ½ teaspoon baking powder
- ¼ teaspoon baking soda
- ½ teaspoon kosher salt
- 1 ½ cups sugar
- 2 teaspoons pure vanilla extract
- 3 large eggs, at room temperature
- 1 cup whole milk

1. Preheat oven to 350 degrees. Butter the pan(s), line the bottoms with parchment, butter again, and dust with flour, tapping out the excess. (For cupcakes, there is no need for parchment or re-buttering.) In a medium bowl, whisk together the flour, baking powder, baking soda, and salt; set aside.

2. Using an electric mixer, beat the butter and sugar on medium-high until fluffy, 2 to 3 minutes. Beat in the vanilla, then the eggs one at a time, scraping down the sides of the bowl as necessary.

3. Reduce mixer speed to low. Add the flour mixture in 3 additions and the milk in 2 additions, beginning and ending with the flour mixture. Mix just until combined (do not over mix).

4. Transfer the batter to the prepared pan(s) and bake until a toothpick inserted in the center comes out clean (*see baking times, below). Cool the cake(s) in the pan(s) for 15 minutes, then turn out onto rack(s) to cool completely.

*Baking times: For two 8-inch rounds: 25 to 30 minutes. For two 9-inch rounds: 22 to 25 minutes. For one 9-by-13-inch rectangle: 25 to 30 minutes. For 24 cupcakes: 15 to 20 minutes.

Yield: 2 8-inch cakes, 2 9-inch cakes, 1 9x13-inch rectangle cake, or 24 cupcakes.

Afterword

Have a challenge or two or fifty? Who doesn't?
If you want to learn more about how to cook your way through
your life's challenges, contact Debra (she always writes back)
at www.cookyourselfhappy.com or www.debraborden.com
and follow her on YouTube and Twitter @soustherapist
to learn more about upcoming books and events.

Afterword

About the Author

Debra Borden is a Licensed Clinical Social Worker in New York and New Jersey and the author of two novels, *Lucky Me* and *A Little Bit Married*. Her essays and articles have appeared in *Women's Health Magazine* and *The New York Times*. This book is the first in the COOK YOURSELF HAPPY™ series.

Debra received an English degree from The University of Michigan and a Masters in Social Work from Fordham University. In addition to counseling, Debra has been a liaison and continues to be a resource for individuals, families, and professionals seeking psychiatric and substance abuse help. She is a pioneer in the field of Cooking Therapy.

Debra lives with her ever-changing but always sustaining Sous family in New York and New Jersey.

For more information, visit www.cookyourselfhappy.com.

CPSIA information can be obtained
at www.ICGtesting.com
Printed in the USA
LVHW05s0320270718
585116LV00007B/197/P